To Maria,

For all your support and understanding.

# Praise for Bielsa = Leeds (2019)

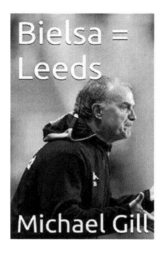

*"I will keep your book forever."*
**-Marcelo Bielsa, July 2019**

*"Worth it for Bielsa's well-thought-out comments."*
-Roger Smith, October 2019 on Amazon UK

*"More like a sit down chat with a good-natured supporter than a highly polished piece of prose."*
-Paul Challen, December 2019 on Amazon Canada

*"Fantastic insight into the Leeds Manager."*
-Cheryl Jagger, April 2020 on Amazon UK

*"Hope another one will follow for this season."*
-Pauline Thompson, April 2020 on Twitter UK

*"Gill analyses the motives, generosity and fine tuning that Bielsa puts into his working life."*
-Craig Minto, June 2020 on Amazon UK

# Contents
## Bielsa Delivers: Leeds Go Home

# Chapter One
## Preparation Points

All the emotions of bereavement were experienced by most United fans after the second play off game. All emotions except, perhaps denial as there was no denying what had happened. We managed to throw away the chance of returning to our rightful home after being two goals ahead in the second leg against Derby County of all teams!

The atmosphere on our supporters' coach on the way back from Elland Road was toxic. I listened to the comments of my companions and wanted to argue with them. But what could I say? We all felt deflated but angry as well. It was almost as though our heroes had deliberately lost the game.

My normal therapy for a result of this nature is to act in a very childish fashion: I reach for my crime novel and block all football thoughts from my mind. Tonight, even this form of solace was not available.

In honour of the occasion that was in it, our coach driver had persuaded his bosses to hire us a luxurious coach with tables that you could sit at and talk to your companions in comfort. This was great on our way to the match, when we were all filled with such hope. On the way back, however, it prevented us from curling up and dying quietly.

Most close seasons are a long boring trial for football fans, but this one was going to seem to last longer than usual. Added to these anxieties was the persistent rumour that Marcelo Bielsa would not be hanging around to witness another season. Although this type of behaviour was at odds with Bielsa's normal routine, the worry persisted.

The Bielsa spotters were out in force. The great man had been seen at Morrisons in Wetherby, and some wag on Twitter claimed to have checked the sell by dates on his shopping! He was also observed with Victor Orta, having a business meeting in the Sky Bar and shortly afterwards in a car showroom.

In his usual thorough way, Bielsa had a series of meetings with his employers and on Tuesday 28th May, Andrea Radrizzani proudly announced that Marcelo would be staying. The white smoke billowed gently from the Vatican chimneys and our worst fear was not realised.

The man himself had returned to Argentina for a well-earned holiday. That is of course, if one assumes that he knows how to rest.

The month of June flew by, but as July dawned upon us, United had signed Jack Harrison up for another year's loan from Manchester City. Helder Costa, the club's number one target had been acquired from Wolves on loan with an option to buy and the promising youngster; Liam McCarron had been signed from Carlisle United.

Central defender Ben White had joined on loan from Brighton. Although untested in the Championship, White had impressed at Newport and Peterborough. He had a reputation for being a ball-playing defender who fitted into Bielsa's philosophy of how a centre back should play.

Probably the best bit of business was the sale of Jack Clarke to Spurs, which saw the teenager immediately return to the Whites on a year's loan.

Rumours abounded about Pontus Jansson. The big Swede had not appeared at Thorpe Arch when the rest of the squad had returned from their holidays.

He had been a favourite at Elland Road since being signed by former boss Garry Monk. Jansson is very emotional and wore his heart on his sleeve and loved celebrating moments of triumph with the fans.

Stories persisted that he was not a team player, that he could be a disruptive influence and that he had refused to return after the break at the same time as the other players.

He had also defied Bielsa in the Aston Villa game the previous season by trying to prevent Adomah from scoring when he had been instructed to allow him through unopposed. Whatever the reasons behind Jansson's fall from grace, it was clear that Bielsa was not a man who would sacrifice principle for convenience.

When it was confirmed that he was no longer required, pandemonium broke out and the fans quickly split into two groups. Many trusted Bielsa and quoted the famous mantra of Billy Bremner: 'Side before self'. Others could not believe that the club would be prepared to allow such an influential player to leave.

However, leave he did! He was soon fixed up with Brentford for a fee in the region of £5.5 million. The club sensibly stayed silent on the matter but the agreed figure and the fact that Brentford were the only club interested spoke volumes.

In mid July, United were back in action away at York City and Guiseley respectively.

**York City 0-5 Leeds United**
10th July, 2019

*Leeds United*
Casilla, Dallas (Hosannah 62), Berardi (Casey 62), Cooper (Struijk 62), Douglas (Jenkins 62), Hernandez (Mujica 62), Forshaw (Gotts 62), McCalmont (Oduor 62), Harrison (McCarron 62), Roofe (Temenuzhkov 62), Bamford (Edmondson 62).

It did not take too long for the more negative fans to point out that Kalvin Phillips was conspicuous by his absence. Last season's lynchpin and most improved player had initially been linked with a move to Aston Villa.

But the fans fears were allayed when it was announced that Phillips would be lining up against Guiseley the following night. Also absent were Ayling, White, Shackleton, Alioski, Klich, Clarke, Costa and Roberts.

Nevertheless, it was a strong side that faced the Minstermen. This was borne out by the performance as United took their neighbours apart. Harrison (2), Hernandez, Roofe and Forshaw piled up the tally of goals and the game was all but over before the entire team (apart from Casilla) was changed just past the hour mark.

**Guiseley 1-2 Leeds United**
11th July, 2019

*Leeds United*
Peacock-Farrell (Miazek 45), Shackleton, White (Kenneh 74), Davis, Alioski (Huggins 86), Bogusz, Phillips, Klich, Stevens, Clarke, Costa.

Guiseley were an entirely different prospect to York and tested United all the way. Their striker, Felix, opened the scoring early in the first half, beating Phillips to the ball after Klich had lost possession near the halfway line.

Alioski was 'in the wars' for much of the game, taking a battering from his opponents. It was the class of the lively Costa that made the difference in the end as he slotted home a fine individual effort, before providing a pinpoint assist for Bogusz.

The giant sixteen-year-old Noah Kenneh was also introduced with around fifteen minutes left and strode around like a veteran. He is definitely one to watch for the future.

Two things help me to get through the summer months. My interest in sport is only there when I can passionately back one of the teams.

Leeds Rhinos have been a great side to watch up until recently. They peaked in the season of 2015 when they conquered all. Since then, they have been in decline, despite taking their last title in 2017.

They were struggling again this time out and faced a real prospect of relegation. This was ironic inasmuch as the Leeds Rugby hierarchy had voted for the straightforward relegation of the bottom club. They were criticised at the time by folks who said that it was fine for them to vote in this way as it was unlikely that the Headingley club would ever find themselves in such a desperate situation!

Thankfully, Richard Agar's men staged a fight back and eventually finished eighth with a team which looked very promising for the following season.

My other summer diversion is Gaelic football. I owe my allegiance to the Mayo team thanks to the influence of my parents, who both hailed from this wild but beautiful part of western Ireland.

Again, Mayo have done well in recent years, reaching All Ireland finals in 2013, 2014, 2016 and 2017. In those latter two years, they lost on each occasion by a single point to Dublin and in 2019, they were defeated by them again in the semis.

The Dublin side are phenomenal and have won the All Ireland finals for the last five years on the trot. They are the only county to achieve this in the history of the competition.

Why do I mention all of this in a book about Marcelo Bielsa? Please have patience with me and carry on reading.

Coverage of Gaelic football has improved tremendously in the UK and at around 6.50pm on Saturday 13th July, I settled down in front of my television with a cold can to watch the Dublin versus Cork match.

Just before the throw in, my phone rang. I did not recognise the number, but the call was being made from inside the country.

"Hello is this Michael?"
"Yes, it is."
"My name is Marcelo Bielsa. You sent me a book. I will keep it forever. In the book you say 'muchas gracias'. I want to say muchas gracias to you."

I was completely speechless.

He went on to say: "I do not speak very good English but there is someone with me who can. Do you want to ask me any questions?"

After stammering like a starstruck schoolboy, I told the interpreter that I had been watching Leeds since 1958 and that I believed that the appointment of Marcelo was one of the best things to happen in the history of the club.

I babbled on about how much he was appreciated (which he knows anyway) and wished him all the best. The conversation lasted for about five minutes but it will always stay in my memory.

I had posted a copy of the book to him at Thorp Arch a few days earlier. The team had already departed for Australia, but Bielsa had stayed behind, going out to join them later. I was not even aware that he was still in the country!

The following Wednesday, Leeds were due to meet their old protagonists, Manchester United, in Perth. Bielsa had decided to take a very limited squad to Australia. In addition to the injured Ayling and Roberts; Costa, Peacock-Farrell, White, Alioski, Klich, Shackleton and Clarke were all left behind in the UK.

No reason for their omission was given, but it was assumed that they needed fitness conditioning or in the case of Costa and White, acclimatisation to the club's methods.

**Manchester United 4-0 Leeds United**
17th July, 2019

*Leeds United*
Casilla, Douglas, Forshaw, Cooper, Roofe, Bamford
(Bogusz 63), Dallas (Hosannah 66), Hernandez
(Stevens 77), Harrison, Phillips, Berardi.

Predictably enough, GREENWOOD (7) opened the
scoring. RASHFORD (27) added a second. JONES
(51) converted a Martial corner. MARTIAL (78)
himself slotted home a penalty after Cooper had
upended the tricky and skilful Chong.

Yes, it was a good drubbing as expected, but what
the score line does not tell is that the Whites played
some great attacking football and were unlucky not
to get at least one consolation goal.

Towards the end of the first half, they threw
everything but the kitchen sink at their Premier
League rivals as the familiar spectre of unconverted
chances returned to haunt them yet again. The team
then flew to Sydney to fulfil a fixture with Western
Sydney Wanderers in their brand new stadium.

**Western Sydney Wanderers 1-2 Leeds United**
20th July, 2019

*Leeds United*
Casilla, Douglas, Cooper, Berardi, Dallas, Phillips,
Bogusz (Oduor 72), Hernandez, Harrison, Roofe
(Stevens 50), Bamford.

United started like a house on fire, with BOGUSZ (9) slamming home a great drive from the edge of the penalty area. A strike which was reminiscent of some of the goals by his fellow countryman, Klich, last season.

Early in the second half, Western Sydney Wanderers were level thanks to YEBOAH (48). As the clock ticked by with more chances missed notably by Bamford and Hernandez before the little Spaniard injected some magic of his own.

At the last gasp, he weaved around the penalty area, beating five men in the process, before planting the ball in the top corner of the net. HERNANDEZ (90+5) brought back memories of Eddie Gray's famous goal against Burnley to conclude the Australia trip in style.

Three days earlier, the players who had been left behind were blended into a side of academy hopefuls to face Tadcaster Albion.

**Tadcaster Albion 1-5 Leeds United**
17th July, 2019

*Leeds United*
Rae, Gotts, White, Alioski (Struijk 71), Jenkins, Klich, Temenuzhkov, Clarke, Costa (Mujica 61), Edmonson.

A mismatched game saw the strong Whites side comfortably beat Tadcaster by five goals to one.

EDMONSON (10), (64) and (75), CLARKE (20) and GOTTS (45) all scored for United, with DAY (49) replying for Albion.

For the first time in many years, United did not hold a curtain raiser at Elland Road and instead, travelled to Serie A side Cagliari, formerly owned by Massimo Cellino.

Of course, our beloved ex-president was no stranger to controversy and looking at Cagliari's crumbling current home it is rather as well that the Italian has no longer any connection to Leeds United.

**Cagliari 1-1 Leeds United**
27th July, 2019

*Leeds United*
Casilla, Davis, Cooper, White, Berardi, Phillips, Klich (Bogusz 65) Forshaw, Costa (Clarke 61), Hernandez, Bamford.

This was never going to be a classic and it looked like Cagliari would fight tooth and nail to hang on to their early lead.

They took the initiative early in the game, when BIRSA (16) gave White the slip on the edge of the penalty area and shot the ball past Kiko Casilla.

After five minutes of the second half, Klich burst into the box to pick up a good through ball from Leif Davis only to be upended.

HERNANDEZ (49) coolly placed the resultant penalty out of Cragno's reach in the Cagliari goal.

Both sides came close, but that was it. Kalvin Phillips picked up a meaningless red card just before the final whistle for a lunge on Pinna.

In a nutshell, United created lots of chances but conversion was once again the problem.

# Chapter Two
## Early Encouragement

A trip to Bristol kicked off United's season, with Lee Johnson once again trotting the old 'Spygate' chestnut out, saying that he and his assistant had considered renting a flat overlooking Leeds United's training ground.

Furthermore, he had organised a public training session for his own side. I sincerely hope that he keeps his job in football because he will never make a living as a stand-up comedian!

**Bristol City 1-3 Leeds United**
4th August, 2019

*Bristol City*
Bentley, Hunt, Kalas, Moore, Dasilva, Pack, Brownhill, Weimann, Palmer (Eliasson 64), O'Dowda (Paterson 63), Diedhiou (Taylor 80).

*Leeds United*
Casilla, Dallas, White, Cooper, Douglas (Alioski 79), Phillips, Hernandez, Forshaw, Klich (Costa 76), Harrison (Davis 85), Bamford.

Attendance: 23,553    Referee: Tim Robinson

United edged their way into the game, playing the kind of football that we have come to know and love. After just over halfway through the first period, HERNANDEZ (26) found the top left corner of the net with an unstoppable strike.

Ben White made an impressive debut, looking cool and composed. His distribution and the speed with which he played the ball out from the back were both superior to that of his predecessor, Pontus Jansson. Kiko Casilla also continued to thrill us with some unconventional goalkeeping.

As the game progressed, United grew in strength. BAMFORD (57) headed home the second after receiving an inch perfect pass from the irrepressible Pablo Hernandez. HARRISON (72) tapped in a third as United coasted to what should have been an easy victory. WEIMANN (79) gave them a wake-up call, but the Whites were in no mood to surrender any more goals.

This was a fine win which has answered a lot of questions, and hopefully Leeds should be set fair for a tilt at the top spots.

**League Position: 1st**

*"I have a lot of confidence with the squad that I have now. We have three players for every position. Even though there are not thirty-three players, we have eighteen players that are good enough to play in three positions differently.*

*Last season, Jack Clarke and Jamie Shackleton became involved and now they are closer to being part of the team. I hope and I am sure at the end of the season there will be two players more to assume the role that Jamie and Jack now have."*

-Marcelo Bielsa

Following United's opening day win, the transfer window drew to its conclusion.

Kemar Roofe, who had one year remaining on his contract departed for Belgian club Anderlecht and Bailey Peacock-Farrell, made the short trip over the Pennines to Burnley.

As well as the financial aspects, Roofe was probably attracted by the prospect of playing in European competitions. In Peacock-Farrell's case, it was hard to see beyond the monetary aspect as his prospects of first team football would hardly be enhanced by his transfer.

United signed French stopper Ilan Meslier from Lorient as a replacement for Bailey Peacock-Farrell. For once, a foreign name wasn't as big a mouthful as an English one!

Eddie Nketiah was also signed on loan from Arsenal on deadline day. This talented youngster was sought by no fewer than 25 different clubs across Europe.

He was due to sign for Bristol City, but Victor Orta convinced both the player and his manager Unai Emery that Eddie should come and work under Bielsa at Leeds. The Robins had already booked his medical and were not pleased by the late development.

*Incoming Players*
Jack Harrison - Manchester City (Loan)
Ben White - Brighton & Hove Albion (Loan)
Liam McCarron - Carlisle United (Undisclosed Fee)
Jack Clarke - Tottenham Hotspur (Loan)
Helder Costa - Wolverhampton Wanderers (Loan)
Rafa Mujica - Barcelona (Free)
Guillermo Amor - Barcelona (Free)
Illan Meslier - Lorient (Loan)
Eddie Nketiah - Arsenal (Loan)

*Outgoing Players*
Paudie O'Connor - Bradford City (Free)
Jay-Roy Grot - Vitesse Arnhem (Loan)
Jack Clarke - Tottenham Hotspur (Undisclosed)
Aapo Halme - Barnsley (Undisclosed)
Lewie Coyle - Fleetwood Town (Loan)
Mallik Wilks - Barnsley (Undisclosed)
Liam Kitching - Forest Green Rovers (Undisclosed)
Pontus Jansson - Brentford (Undisclosed)
Tyler Denton - Stevenage (Undisclosed)
Sam Dalby - Watford (Undisclosed)
Samuel Saiz - Girona (Undisclosed)
Oliver Sarkic - Burton Albion (Free)
Bailey Peacock-Farrell - Burnley (£2.5m)
Yosuke Ideguchi - Osaka (Undisclosed)

Kemar Roofe - Anderlecht (Undisclosed)
Tom Pearce - Wigan Athletic (Undisclosed)
Clarke Oduor - Barnsley (Undisclosed)
Laurens De Bock - Sunderland (Free)
Conor Shaughnessy - Mansfield Town (Loan)
Caleb Ekuban - Trabzonspor (£900,000)
Hadi Sacko - Denizlispor (Undisclosed)
Vurnon Anita - Released

Once again, many surplus players had been moved on and a smaller number acquired. Despite some opinions to the contrary, it was a very satisfactory window for United.

And so, to the first home game. As always it was good to see friendly faces on the coach and all talk of the play off failure was banished.

**Leeds United 1-1 Nottingham Forest**
10th August, 2019

*Leeds United*
Casilla, Dallas, White, Cooper, Douglas, Phillips, Hernandez, Forshaw, Klich (Costa 80), Harrison (Alioski 73), Bamford.

*Nottingham Forest*
Muric, Cash, Dawson, Worrall, Robinson, Watson (Mir 72), Adomah (Ameobi 64), Silva (Sow 57), Semedo, Lolley, Grabban.

Attendance: 35,453    Referee: Robert Jones

An almost full Elland Road spurred the Whites on right from the start. Real chances were few in the opening period, but Bamford and Hernandez both came close.

After the break and more missed chances, HERNANDEZ (59) showed his team mates how things should be done, picking up a fine through ball from Klich, the Spaniard raced through the middle to put the ball beyond the reach of the advancing Muric.

Although Bamford found himself in the right place on a couple of occasions, it looked like it was going to be one of those days when things didn't click for him. Forest seemed to be soaking up the pressure and it was not long before United were made to pay for their profligacy.

The Whites defence which had been immaculate up until this point failed to clear their lines from a rare Forest corner. In the resultant melee, GRABBAN (77) gratefully slid the ball home at the far post.

Despite battering the Forest goal for the remainder of the game, United were unable to find the net for a second time.

**League Position: 3rd**

*"We lost two points so we are disappointed with the result but the team are growing and not losing the ball easily. We didn't receive any counter attacks today. They scored from a corner which we gave away. We had a lot of chances to put the ball in the box from the sides.*

*We had players in the box waiting for the ball. But of course, this is something we can improve.*
*It's very difficult to be a referee, I don't know if it was a penalty but we had enough ways to solve the game without this."*

-Marcelo Bielsa

Singaporean businessman Peter Lim, who owns Spanish side Valencia, joined with former Manchester United players Ryan Giggs, Gary and Phil Neville, Paul Scholes and Nicky Butt to acquire Salford City in 2014.

They were later joined by David Beckham, never one to miss a publicity opportunity.

After winning the play off final last year, Salford City joined the Football League and when The Whites were drawn against them in the Carabao Cup, it was a fixture which attracted the interest of many United fans.

Visitors can be forgiven for being confused as to where or even what Salford is. The truth is that the locals are equally confused.

The area is variously described as being a city, a borough of Greater Manchester, or a collection of boroughs which include Eccles, Worsley, Irlam, Cadishead, Swinton and Pendlebury.

Salford was given 'city' status in 1926 and in those days was synonymous with huge cotton mills, dole and poverty, but at least the residents in those days had some idea of where they lived.

My own earliest recollection of this mythical place was watching old black and white movies on television during wet and miserable Sunday afternoons.

'Love on the Dole' (1941) and 'Hobson's Choice' (1954) come to mind. In the days when these films were made, household names like Deborah Kerr, Charles Laughton and John Mills struggled to adapt their cut-glass accents to imitate the flat vowels of Lancashire. Northern folk were usually portrayed as likeable simpletons and trouble at t'Mill was never far away.

Another famous son of Salford was the painter LS Lowry, whose excellent but gloomy paintings portrayed the area's dark satanic mills and factories. The 'city' was also celebrated in Ewan MacColl's song 'Dirty Old Town.' To add to the confusion, a lot of people think that the song is about Dublin.

Today, the conglomeration of Salford spreads out to the north and west from Manchester city centre. Salford City Football Club itself is on the eastern fringes of this confusing area, very close to the fine Jewish neighbourhood of Whitefield where I have enjoyed many a plate of gefilte fish and latkes.

Unlike a lot of Leeds fans, I have nothing against the city of Manchester itself, because I have enjoyed far too many good nights out there for that to be the case. Therefore, on the date of our Carabao Cup tie with Salford, I made my way to Manchester, sorry, Salford for the game.

Having a little time to spare, I used National Express which was by far the cheapest mode of transport available. I usually board the coach at Milton Keynes and as it has started at Victoria and probably called at Golders Green bus station on the way, it is almost always nearly full.

This is the signal for me to adopt my National Express travel mode. The rules are:

- Have your ticket ready to be scrutinised by the (usually rude) driver.
- Avoid eye contact with everyone.
- Stride purposely along the coach until you find a seat next to a little old man or little old woman. If you hesitate and look for a seat to yourself, you are likely to end up seated next to a 22 stone bodybuilder with a personal freshness problem.

- Do not be put off by people who leave their bag on the spare seat. Awaken them politely but firmly, even if they appear to have passed away!
- Never attempt to use the toilet.
- If the coach stops for a comfort break, return promptly. Otherwise they WILL leave you at the Motorway Services.

I managed to get off the bus without incident at Chorlton Street Manchester and walked around the corner to the once proud Britannia Hotel. Nowadays, the hotel resembles an elderly good time girl who is struggling to maintain her attractiveness.

I had managed to acquire an ensuite but windowless room for £39 (room only). It was clean, adequate and the shower worked. I then dumped my bag and headed over Portland Street to the Circus Tavern. The bar is a Manchester institution which claims to be the smallest pub in England.

The pint of Tetley's was magnificent, but the talk was of Old Trafford. Because of the pub's size and layout, it is impossible to shrink into a corner and play with your phone. You MUST engage!

I make a rule of never discussing politics, religion or Manchester United under any circumstances especially when drink is taken and so I reluctantly gulped the rest of my pint down and repaired two doors away to the Grey Horse, a much more suitable venue for the discerning Leeds supporter.

I then enjoyed some very good dim sum at the New China City, before making my way by bus to the Peninsula Stadium.

At the ground, I bought a programme, the cover of which depicted a Campbell's soup tin in the style of Andy Warhol, whose works have been exhibited at The Lowry Gallery, Salford.

Just in case you haven't already guessed it, the gallery is nowhere near the stadium. In fact, you need to go back through Manchester to get there!

**Salford City 0-3 Leeds United**
13th August, 2019

*Salford City*
Neal, Piergianni, J Jones, Pond, Maynard, Threlkeld (Gaffney 62), Towell, Whitehead, Touray, Beesley (Lloyd-McGoldrick 69), Dieseruvwe (Rooney 70).

*Leeds United*
Casilla, Berardi, White, Davis, Alioski (Harrison 78), Phillips, Costa, Shackleton, Klich, Clarke (McCalmont 70), Nketiah (Bamford 78).

Attendance: 4,518     Referee: Keith Stroud

United started the game in their usual sprightly fashion but it was clear that Salford had set themselves up to defend and frustrate.
Patience was needed and United applied their patience in their usual professional manner.

Salford had a couple of breakaway chances, most notably when Leif Davis cleared off the line from Towell. Leeds steadily worked their way into the game with Kalvin Phillips and Jack Clarke trying long range efforts.

It was a touch of sheer class that gave United the lead. Jamie Shackleton sent Helda Costa down the right and his defence-splitting cross left NKETIAH (43) with the simple task of tapping the ball into an empty net. The Arsenal loanee had already endeared himself to the travelling supporters as chants of 'Eddie, Eddie' rang around the small stadium.

Early in the second half, BERARDI (50) flicked in a shot from the near post as a result of a corner. The good-natured threat of a pitch invasion from our fans was not realised despite the rarity of this goal - not just Berardi, but Berardi from a corner!

KLICH (58) put the game beyond Salford's reach with a rasping shot into the top corner. The game was a professionally executed task against lower league opposition. Efficient without being spectacular.

*"Every game is an important game. I know we have different levels of games, it's not the same for one league game when you are trying to fight for points, but games are all very important.*

*One of the targets is to have more players involved than the players are usually playing. This type of scenario helps as every player can show what they are able to do."*

-Marcelo Bielsa

Salford City's programme cover.

The following morning, having a little bit of time to spare, I decided to look for a nice simple cafe that would be able to serve me a freshly cooked full English breakfast.

I headed in the opposite direction to the Gay Village, with its trendy and therefore expensive eateries. I was not after hand-crafted eggs benedict drizzled with kir royale, but rather for something greasier and more substantial.

My search took me past Piccadilly Gardens and was not going too well. Eventually I found a sandwich bar which advertised the very delicacy that I was looking for.

The only problem was that the furniture consisted of a shelf in front of the window and one high stool. The stool was occupied by a man of indeterminate age. He wore what used to be called a rally jacket and a pair of scruffy jogging pants. I asked him where I could find a cafe where I could sit down and eat my breakfast.

"Nay lad, there is one a few streets away but it's not a patch on the grub here. Order it up and I'll get off the stool when your food is served. Jean, there's a customer here."

I thanked him and took his advice. At this point, I noticed that he was watching the woman in a somewhat furtive manner, clearly waiting until she disappeared around the back to prepare my food.

Once she had gone, he turned to me and said:

"I used to love a fry up, but I'm not allowed to eat them now since I had my operation. It plays havoc wi' my guts you see."

He then went on to describe in graphic detail how this condition affected his digestion.

Pointing to the kitchen, he said:

"She plays hell with me for talking about it, 'cause she says it puts people off their food."

He obviously felt that having given up his seat for me, that he was entitled to give me the gory details. Thankfully Jean arrived shortly and I was spared the tour of his large and small intestines. What I have to say is that he was 100% right about the food. It was absolutely excellent.

The stretch between Wigan North Western station is not noted for pubs, much less decent beer. Since the closure of the 'Orwell' on Wigan Pier some years ago, the walk from the station to the ground has been an unrelenting slog past car showrooms, a supermarket and a retail park. That is unless you take the 'scenic' route by the canal and industrial estate. Fortunately, there is one notable exception.

The wonderful 'Wigan Central' is situated just around the corner from North Western station.

It is housed in two railway arches and is well worth a visit. The concept is bang up-to-date with the latest craft beers, ciders and gins, but the pub has its feet firmly planted on the ground.

There is a great selection of cask ales led by local brewers Prospect from Standish, but has contributions from Yorkshire and the Midlands as well. If you can't find a beer to suit you in here, then you should change your tipple. The scotch eggs and pork pies provided are of a superior quality also.

Should you linger in this drinkers haven too long, you can always get a taxi to the ground and avoid being tempted to take a dip in the filthy canal as I saw a couple of Leeds fans doing on this blisteringly hot day.

**Wigan Athletic 0-2 Leeds United**
17th August, 2019

*Wigan Athletic*
Marshall, Byrne, Dunkley, Fox, Robinson, Morsy, Williams, Massey (Enobakhare 65), Evans, Jacobs (Lowe 65), Moore (Naismith 83).

*Leeds United*
Casilla, Dallas, White, Cooper, Douglas, Phillips, Hernandez, Forshaw (Shackleton 90), Klich (Costa 76), Harrison, Bamford.

Attendance: 14,819    Referee: Andy Madley

United had a simple task ahead of them and they executed it perfectly. For the second time in a few months, Wigan were reduced to ten players when Joe Williams was sent off for a second bookable offence after twenty minutes.

This time, United were in no mood to surrender their advantage and BAMFORD (34) put them ahead with a tap in. The big striker pounced on the opportunity after the ball cannoned out of the post from an Adam Forshaw header.

Once again, Kalvin Phillips and Adam Forshaw bossed the midfield and Jack Harrison teased and tormented the Wigan defence with an energetic performance which showed clearly how the Manchester City loanee has improved his game under Marcelo Bielsa's tutelage.

Just thirty minutes after his first goal, BAMFORD (65) bundled in another scrappy effort after Wigan failed to clear a Barry Douglas corner. Two ugly strikers' goals taken with ease can only increase Bamford's confidence after he had come in for some unfair criticism from some quarters.

If there was one small niggle with United's performance, it was sometimes their build up was too elaborate as they tried to walk the ball into the net. However, this was another of last season's ghosts laid by this determined outfit.

**League Position: 1st**

*"It was a fair result; we could have scored more goals. Playing with one more player is an important advantage. It was a game full of free kicks but today, we played more calmly in defence than usual. The performance of the team is increasing day by day and game by game."*

-Marcelo Bielsa

The next fixture brought back very painful and raw memories for United fans. Last season's visit to Griffin Park was the fixture which finally took away all hope of automatic promotion. The Whites, of course, lost 2-0 and the previous match back in the autumn ended in a controversial draw.

Added to the game this time was the return of prodigal son Pontus Jansson and a sell-out crowd.

**Leeds United 1-0 Brentford**
21st August, 2019

*Leeds United*
Casilla, Dallas (Berardi 78), White, Cooper, Alioski, Phillips, Hernandez (Nketiah 77), Forshaw, Klich, Harrison (Costa 65), Bamford.

*Brentford*
Raya, Jeanvier, Jansson, Pinnock (Marcondes 89), Dalsgaard, Jensen, Norgaard, Henry, Mbeumo (Dasilva 67), Watkins, Canos (Benrahma 79).

Attendance: 35,004    Referee: Andy Davies

Jansson captained the Bees, but United fans were more worried about their own defensive options with Cooper and Douglas both doubtful owing to injury. In the event, Cooper made the team but Douglas didn't and was replaced by the capable, but eccentric Alioski.

Despite their attacking reputation, it was clear that Brentford were going to 'park the bus' and rely on breakaways. Nevertheless, the side from West London nearly took the lead after 23 minutes, when new signing Bryan Mbeumo lashed the ball against the post after catching Stuart Dallas napping.

United started the second half with two corners which were cleared as was another Forshaw effort from the edge of the box. The onslaught continued with three more corners and a Pablo Hernandez shot which narrowly cleared the bar.

Klich then had a shot blocked by what appeared to be an arm. A furious Stuart Dallas was then booked for dissent as he tried to remonstrate with referee Andy Davis, who is unlikely to be ennobled the freedom of Elland Road any time soon.

This incident would have been even more controversial, had Ollie Watkins taken full advantage of the resultant breakaway. As it was, he shot the ball wide. Helder Costa then replaced Jack Harrison and almost immediately set Stuart Dallas up. The Irishman's shot, however, was high wide and not too handsome.

With only 13 minutes left, Eddie Nketiah replaced
Pablo Hernandez and joined Patrick Bamford
upfront. The Arsenal loanee had a shot deflected
and very shortly after this found the target.

Klich had sent Costa away with a fine through ball.
The former Wolves man sent a low cross in and to
the delight of the Elland Road crowd, (NKETIAH
81) was in the right place to slot the ball home.

The young striker has excellent positioning skills
and one of his mentors, Ian Wright, was among the
crowd and celebrated a Leeds goal for the first time
in his career.

**League Position: 1st**

*"We deserved to win the game because we
dominated the game. We didn't create a lot of
chances, but we created enough chances to make a
difference. It was a physically demanding game and
we took control in the best moment of the game.*

*Helder Costa is a balanced player who can play on
both sides and Eddie Nketiah can make an impact
in the middle. We defended well and our opponents
did not have enough clear chances."*

-Marcelo Bielsa

# Chapter Three
## Commendable Camp

Around this time, the documentary film 'Take Us Home' was released. It was narrated by Whites fan and actor Russell Crowe.

The 'fly on the wall' series charted United's progress during last season in six episodes and was available on Amazon Prime. The good part was that you could join Prime, watch the film and then cancel your subscription, or so I am told.

It received a mixed reception as some fans just found the ending too painful to watch. I watched five episodes and then waited until after the Brentford game before watching the last episode, believing that I would be in a sufficiently positive frame of mind to suffer the agonies of the ending of the season's dream.

CEO, Angus Kinnear, described the last episode being like watching a car crash in slow motion.

Since then, I have urged anybody who would listen to me to watch the film. It is done impressively and above all gives you an insight into the personalities of the characters involved.

From the likeable and committed Radrizzani, to the passionate and emotional Victor Orta, to the calm and collected Kinnear.

Any doubts that a fan might have about the collective commitment of these guys to the club would be dispelled by watching this great biopic.

Only one man continues to remain a mystery. Of course, I refer to the enigmatic Marcelo Bielsa, but nobody expected him to open his heart to the public. To be fair to the producers of the film, they never made such a claim either.

A trip to Stoke is always a pleasure. Last season, I sampled the delights of the famous Victorian pub, The Glebe, owned by Joules of Market Drayton.

This time around, I visited the White Star owned by the Titanic Brewery of Stoke, which is also pleasant and close to the shuttle bus which goes to straight to Stoke City's ground.

With no fewer than ten cask ales available, it would definitely take a few visits to do this place justice while maintaining a reasonable standard of health and fitness!

**Stoke City 0-3 Leeds United**
24th August, 2019

*Stoke City*
Federici, Collins, Carter-Vickers (Allen 73),
Lindsay, Edwards, Cousins, Etebo, Clucas,
McClean, Duffy (Hogan 60), Gregory (Ince 73).

*Leeds United*
Casilla, Dallas, Berardi, White, Alioski, Phillips,
Hernandez (Costa 80), Harrison, Klich (Shackleton
85), Forshaw, Bamford (Nketiah 74).

Attendance: 24,090    Referee: Darren England

The corresponding fixture last season was Nathan
Jones's first win as Stoke City manager. He had
enjoyed considerable success as manager of Luton
Town and this was a big step up for him.

The win over Leeds was so important to him that he
commissioned a huge photographic mural which
depicted his celebrations surrounded by the team.

Prior to this match, things were somewhat different.
Nathan Jones played what is often the beleaguered
manager's final throw of the dice. He publicly
berated his players in the media before making six
changes for this game.

In the first half, he cut an animated figure, prancing
around his technical area like a manic marionette.

Just before half time, he slowed down and dropped his shoulders, just like his players did.

The shoulder dropping was caused by Stuart Dallas. Pablo Hernandez, who had been having a quiet afternoon, sent a sublime through pass over from the left side of the pitch. This was latched on to by DALLAS (42) after a perfectly timed run, before the Northern Ireland international smashed the ball into the net.

In the second half, United continued where they had left off. ALIOSKI (50) enjoyed a simple tap in after good work from Patrick Bamford.

Another precisely weighted pass from Hernandez found Alioski, whose shot from a tight angle was beaten away by Adam Federici into the path of BAMFORD (66).

The big striker gleefully found the net with a half volley to effectively end any resistance that Stoke might be likely to offer. United could have added to their tally with close efforts from Jack Harrison, Helda Costa and Adam Forshaw.

As for Nathan Jones, he disappeared from the technical area altogether and stayed sat on the bench except when supervising substitutions.

**League Position: 1st**

*"We are playing with the same ideas as last season but losing the ball less. We are spending more time with the ball than without it and we are not losing the ball very easily.*

*We are suffering less counter attacks. This is the same idea of the team and more natural behaviours in the team. It is always positive to get points but we must be calm to analyse the future. It is very difficult to predict what will happen."*

-Marcelo Bielsa

One event took place in August which symbolised all the progress that United had made under Marcelo Bielsa.

The following Tuesday, the Whites were at home to Stoke City in the Carabao Cup, three days after demolishing the Potters in the Championship.

This was not an attractive fixture by any stretch of the imagination and in recent years would have drawn an attendance of around eleven thousand with only half of the ground being open.

As it was, the fixture drew an amazing gate in excess of 30,000.

**Leeds United (4) 2-2 (5) Stoke City**
27th August, 2019

*Leeds United*
Casilla, Berardi, Douglas, Davis, Phillips,
Shackleton (Forshaw 45), McCalmont (White 45),
Costa, Clarke (Harrison 45) Bogusz, Nketiah.

*Stoke City*
Butland, Smith, Carter-Vickers, Batth, Martins Indi,
Ward, Woods (Duffy 90), Clucas, Ince (Cousins 85),
Vokes, Campbell (Etebo 70).

Attendance: 30,002    Referee: Oliver Langford

United fielded a very young side against Stoke. On
paper, Stoke had a very experienced and strong line
up, but was this Nathan Jones's attempt to field a
strong side or was he keeping the bad boys in
detention after school until they mended their ways?
Or had Stoke decided to appoint another head
teacher? We may never know.

After a lively start and several even encounters,
including Eddie Nketiah hitting the bar with
Butland beaten, experience and muscle allowed
Stoke to take the advantage.

A set piece led to the first goal as BATTH (39) rose
above the Leeds defence to head home a corner.
Five minutes later, VOKES (44) doubled the
visitor's lead after good work by Tyrese Campbell.

Bielsa brought on the 'big guns' for the second half as White, Forshaw and Harrison replaced Clarke, Shackleton and McCalmont. The refreshed line up soon burst into action, roared on by the Elland Road faithful. Butland fluffed a clearance allowing NKETIAH (67) to pull one back for United.

With the crowd urging the Whites on and the clock running down, COSTA (81) slotted in an equaliser from a finely executed cross from Leif Davis.

As per the new rules, no extra time was played and so the game went straight to penalties. Player after player on both sides stepped up to the mark and buried the ball in routine fashion, before Jack Harrison hit the post and the game was over.

The crowd had enjoyed a cracking evening's entertainment and were not slow to applaud the Whites and even chanted Harrison's name as his colleagues consoled him.

*"The team played better in the second half than the first but overall, we didn't play with enough clarity. We played much better in the second half. We had a physical difference in the team after the break."*

-Marcelo Bielsa

**Leeds United 0-1 Swansea City**
31st August, 2019

*Leeds United*
Casilla, Dallas, White, Cooper, Alioski (Douglas 83), Phillips, Hernandez, Klich (Costa 71), Forshaw, Harrison, Bamford (Nketiah 61).

*Swansea City*
Woodman, Roberts, van der Hoorn, Rodon, Bidwell, Fulton, Grimes, Ayew (Byers 85), Dhanda (Routledge 63), Celina, Baston (Surridge 63).

Attendance: 34,935    Referee: Darren Bond

Swansea were unquestionably the best team that United had faced all season. They were well organised in defence and fast to move the ball forward and consequently, they tested the Whites throughout the game.

You did feel, though, that United would break through as they played their usual game and took the action to the Swans.

As Leeds battled away, the home fans became quieter, perhaps sensing that it was going to be one of those days where you didn't go home in a happy frame of mind.

But what the heck! A draw wouldn't be too bad would it? Amidst the strangely quiet Elland Road, you even began to hear a couple of stanzas of 'Hymns and Arias' before the home fans reasserted their dominance and made some noise again.

It was all to no avail though, as veteran substitute ROUTLEDGE (90) spoiled the party when he converted a corner.

An ungenerous four minutes of added time was awarded, shortly before referee Darren Bond brought the game to a close. An undeserved first defeat to take with us into the international break.

**League Position: 3rd**

*"The individual performance of the players was positive. Our players played a little under the level that they have. We had the ball constantly. We defended well.*

*We created enough chances to deserve two or three goals. The chances that the opponent had was in relation to the corners and more from the second balls after the corners. We had a high possession of the ball. We attacked with calm. This is the analysis of the game."*

-Marcelo Bielsa

The most significant event of the season's first international break involved Kalvin Phillips.

The 'Yorkshire Pirlo' signed a new five year contract which ties him to the club until 2024. After his graduation from the academy, he became a very useful and promising midfield player.

Before Marcelo Bielsa had even met Phillips, he had studied extensive footage of him from the 2017-2018 season. As soon as the Argentine arrived at Thorpe Arch, he set about building the team around his young protégé.

Phillips just could not get enough of his mentor's coaching methods and over a short period of time blossomed into one of the finest midfield players in the Championship. This fact was evidenced by the admission from Andrea Radrizzani that the club had turned down summer offers for Phillips which were well in excess of £20million.

This reassuring news was promptly followed by new contracts for Liam Cooper and Stuart Dallas. They gratefully accepted five and four year deals respectively.

Andrea Radrizzani realised that he wasn't taking much of a risk by offering these expensive extensions, as it was a fact that Bielsa had increased the value of his prized assets by tens of millions of pounds.

On the Saturday of the international break, I took a trip to Colchester to see them play Walsall and tick another away ground off my list.

I wandered towards the town centre from the station before being 'sucked in' to the excellent Victoria Inn. I had done my research and so I knew that the shuttle bus to the ground stopped right outside the front door of the pub.

The landlord is a Yorkshireman and one of the beers available was 'Yorkshire Embassy Blonde' from Colchester Brewery. I tried a couple of pints of this and was not disappointed.

The disappointment came later, in conversation with some Walsall fans. When I mentioned the shuttle bus, they invited me to check 'Google' again.

I did and realised that the entry was from 2016. The bus was no longer in service. Nevertheless, I joined them along with some helpful locals, who pointed us in the right direction. As for the game, it was of course, a goalless draw.

The first game of 'proper' football after the break was away to Barnsley, with a 12.30 Sunday kick off on 'police advice'.

I travelled with Thames Valley Whites in their double decker bus. As usual, Steve Griffin was on hand to keep everybody in order.

**Barnsley 0-2 Leeds United**
15th September, 2019

*Barnsley*
Collins, Cavare, Andersen, Halme, Williams
(Pinillos 71), Sibbick, Mowatt, Brown (Bahre 79),
Woodrow, Thomas (Thiam 67), Wilks.

*Leeds United*
Casilla, Dallas, White, Cooper, Alioski, Phillips,
Hernandez, Shackleton, Klich (Berardi 90),
Harrison (Costa 45), Bamford (Nketiah 70).

Attendance: 17,598    Referee: Keith Stroud

Barnsley proved to be very worthy and feisty
opponents. They certainly didn't look like
relegation candidates. They were tight in defence
and quick on the counter, and Kiko Casilla certainly
earned his wages.

Tykes goalkeeper, Brad Collins, had a busy first half
himself making good saves from Patrick Bamford
and Pablo Hernandez. Mallik Wilks had been
putting himself about, clearly relishing the prospect
of facing his former employers.

Patrick Bamford managed to find the back of the
net early in the second half, but it was ruled offside.
Once again, it was Eddie Nketiah who made the
difference though. Just when the Whites had
seemed to be battering themselves against a brick
wall, the Arsenal loanee came up with the goods.

Helder Costa had replaced Jack Harrison at half time and Nketiah had replaced the luckless Bamford on 70 minutes. Costa, who was proving to be a scourge of the Barnsley defence, drew a free kick. Kalvin Phillips sent a defence-splitting ball into the penalty area and NKETIAH (84) made no mistake, volleying in from close range.

Just five minutes later, Nketiah was involved in the action again. Former Leeds youngster Aapo Halme had been having a torrid afternoon trying to contain Bamford. He held the Leeds striker in so many close embraces that there was some question of them announcing their engagement at Christmas.

Not having many romantic inclinations, most Leeds fans would have preferred to see the young Finn sent off! The quicksilver Nketiah slipped in behind the Barnsley defence and this time, Halme transferred his clumsy 'affections' to the Arsenal loanee, with the referee pointing to the penalty spot.

KLICH (89) stepped up and calmly dispatched the resultant spot kick, leaving the game beyond doubt.

**League Position: 1st**

*"Eddie has different characteristics and in a match like that, he is a good option. Some players are involved in play a lot before creating chances.*

*Nketiah is more involved at the end of the action but he has good characteristics to combine with his team mates to give us these options. He is a striker who can score goals. For me he is the complete player."*

-Marcelo Bielsa

**Leeds United 1-1 Derby County**
21st September, 2019

*Leeds United*
Casilla, Dallas, White, Cooper, Alioski, Phillips, Hernandez (Douglas 73), Shackleton, Klich, Harrison (Costa 58), Bamford (Nketiah 79).

*Derby County*
Roos, Lowe, Keogh, Clarke, Malone, Huddlestone, Bielik (Paterson 61), Waghorn, Holmes, Jozefzoon (Knight 83), Marriott (Martin 73).

Attendance: 34,741    Referee: Oliver Langford

Once again, the Whites failed to capitalise on their dominance at Elland Road. For a change, United's goal came early in the match and the crowd began to wonder if the day when they were going to put on a gala performance had finally arrived.

Yes, it was an own goal but one that came because of the relentless pressure that Leeds were subjecting Derby to.

Kalvin Phillips once again sent a powerful but perfect free kick to Patrick Bamford, who sent the ball across the goalmouth to Stuart Dallas who smashed the ball towards goal. Roos could only snatch at it and the ball ricocheted off the unfortunate LOWE (20) and into the net.

United failed to add to their tally of goals by half time as they missed a plethora of chances, with the Derby goal coming under a prolonged and sustained battering. Patrick Bamford had worked very hard, putting himself about and giving Richard Keogh and company a very hard time.

He received his just desserts when he muscled his way through a group of Derby defenders only to have his legs whipped away from him. The referee pointed to the spot and last week's hero Klich placed the ball down and stepped up confidently.

His effort was not dissimilar to the one that he scored at Barnsley, except that it rolled to the wrong side of the post. Most observers felt that this would have been the 'coup de grace' for the rapidly tiring Derby team.

Instead of that, it gave them new energy and a sense of foreboding fell over Elland Road. The Whites fans' worst fears were realised when MARTIN (90+2) broke their hearts after converting a pass from Paterson. Another draw which felt like defeat was worsened by Rams manager Phillip Cocu claiming that his game plan had worked!

**League Position: 1st**

*"This has happened a lot of times to us but today was the worst. They shot once all match. We created ten, maybe twelve chances. We played sixty minutes very good but the last fifteen minutes was flat. We couldn't control the end of the match.*

*When we lose a point this way it's difficult to admit reasons why. But we started to play long, rather than line to line."*

-Marcelo Bielsa

Two days later, Bielsa and his team received the prestigious FIFA Fair Play Award.

This award was bestowed upon them in recognition of their actions during the match against Aston Villa in April 2019. This was the occasion when Bielsa ordered his players to allow Villa to 'walk' the ball into the Leeds goal from the halfway line after the Whites had been awarded a goal themselves.

The play had stopped owing to the referee's indecision and the Leeds players had rightly played on instead of acknowledging the injury of Jonathan Kodjia. At no time had the referee blown his whistle, it was not a head injury and Kodjia recovered.

Because Klich kept on playing and scored, the Villa bench erupted but the referee pointed to the centre circle, indicating that the goal had been allowed.

After consulting with his backroom staff, Bielsa ordered captain Liam Cooper to allow Adomah to walk the ball into the Leeds goal unopposed. Everyone apart from Jansson complied, but the Swede was too late to prevent the goal.

The result of the game was 1-1, but a win would have made no difference as United had already booked their ticket to the play offs.

The ceremony for the awards took place in Milan. Bielsa did not attend personally, but captain Liam Cooper and fitness coach Benoit Delaval were sent to accept the award on his behalf. Delaval read the statement below which had been written by Bielsa.

*"When choosing how to act, the most difficult thing is not to choose between right and wrong but to accept the consequences of doing what corresponds. While there are immediate effects, the important thing is to consider how we will feel when time passes and we review our behaviour."*

Regular Leeds observers were not surprised at the reaction, with very few representatives of fellow English clubs offering any praise.

Frank Lampard expressed his 'surprise' and various other members of the 'great and the good' offered their snide comments, seemingly unable or unwilling to show any class at all.

Once again, the EFL establishment showed their true feelings towards Leeds United.

# Chapter Four
## Luckless London

The next match was a trip to Charlton Athletic, who were managed by former Leeds favourite and 'bad boy' Lee Bowyer. Bowyer had mellowed with maturity, but had lost none of the drive and enthusiasm of his youth. He was writing another chapter for the club where he had first made his name, getting them promoted from the third tier.

This fixture is always a pleasure to attend as it involves a pre-match pint and some interesting food in Borough Market.

**Charlton Athletic 1-0 Leeds United**
28th September, 2019

*Charlton Athletic*
Phillips, Solly, Lockyer, Sarr, Purrington, Pratley, Cullen, Leko, Williams (Aneke 56), Gallagher (Pearce 86), Bonne (Field 82).

*Leeds United*
Casilla, Dallas, White, Cooper, Alioski (Nketiah 45), Phillips, Costa, Shackleton (Forshaw 45), Klich, Harrison, Bamford (Roberts 69).

Attendance: 21,808    Referee: John Brooks

Until this match, United had won six away games in succession and had often looked more comfortable away from the highly expectant Elland Road crowd. Things were about to change, however.

Leeds started the game with four corners within a couple of minutes and finished the game in the same way. In between, they were awarded another five and as usual were able to boast possession of more than 70%.

The familiar story of missed chances and wayward shooting was augmented by a scrappy goal which came from one of the two corners which Charlton were awarded. The goal came just after the half hour mark when BONNE (32) slid the ball into the bottom right hand corner of the Leeds net.

Fair play to Lee Bowyer's men though on this showing, what they lacked in finesse, they more than made up for in effort.

United were still struggling with their finishing. Many of the 'quick fix' merchants among the United fanbase believed that the introduction of Helder Costa and Eddie Nketiah would solve all the scoring problems.

Helder Costa started and Eddie Nketiah joined the fray after half time, but the Whites still couldn't find the net.

Adam Forshaw was also drafted in and forgotten man Tyler Roberts replaced Patrick Bamford, who was withdrawn after a petulant foul which earned him a yellow card.

After the final whistle was blown, Lee Bowyer came over to the Leeds end and saluted the fans. Although most were disappointed, this gesture was appreciated. It's a wonder whether he would still feel like doing it after he brings his team to Elland Road, if United have wreaked their revenge.

**League Position: 4th**

*"The difference between the two sides was big. We didn't impose our superiority and that was the reason for what happened. They had one shot and scored one goal. We had possession and controlled the game. Our players were better than their players. We didn't underestimate but we had more resources on the pitch."*

-Marcelo Bielsa

One of the least appealing aspects of a trip by train to Charlton is the awful queue for the train which can sometimes take up to an hour. This was once again avoided by visiting the excellent and reasonably priced Dragon and Phoenix Chinese Restaurant. It opens at 5pm which is perfect and a comforting Cantonese meal washed down with a couple of cold beers can help to remove the bitter taste of an undeserved defeat.

**Leeds United 1-0 West Bromwich Albion**
1st October, 2019

*Leeds United*
Casilla, Dallas, White, Cooper (Berardi 34),
Alioski, Phillips, Costa, Shackleton (Roberts 45)
(Ayling 75), Klich, Harrison, Bamford (Roberts 69).

*West Bromwich Albion*
Johnstone, Furlong, Ajayi, Bartley, Ferguson,
Livermore (Edwards 82), Sawyers, Phillips
(Krovinovic 62), Pereira, Diangana, Robson-Kanu
(Zohore 62).

Attendance: 34,648    Referee: David Coote

West Brom came to town as leaders of the
Championship, which ended in United leapfrogging
them to take the top spot.

The Baggies were unquestionably the most attack-
minded side seen at Elland Road this season,
enjoying 52% of the possession in this open and
exciting match.

They appeared to be very dangerous on the break
and it was from a counter that they almost took the
lead. While Leeds were appealing for a penalty after
a Dallas shot appeared to be blocked by a
defender's hand, the Baggies broke and Robson-
Kanu was presented with a golden opportunity
which he hit tamely towards Kiko Casilla.

West Brom were also racking up a series of yellow cards as Leeds piled on the pressure. Even former United favourite Kyle Bartley was booed as he made a despairing lunge at Patrick Bamford.

There was a scare for the Whites just after half an hour, as Cooper had to retire with an injury. He was replaced by the ever-reliable Gaetano Berardi.

The goal, when it came was pure 'Bielsaball' as Klich, Costa and Shackleton were all involved before Jack Harrison played it across the area to Alioski, whose shot nicked BARTLEY (38) slightly on its way to the net.

In the second half, Tyler Roberts replaced the injured Jamie Shackleton. After twenty-five minutes, Roberts was himself replaced as Bielsa sought to prop up the United defence and withstand the West Brom fightback.

When the final whistle was blown, the relief around the ground could be almost tasted. United had beaten arguably the best team in the division and they showed that they could slug it out in the rare games where they don't enjoy superior possession.

**League Position: 1st**

*"It was a big, big effort from the team. We tried to manage the match, but at the end West Brom's creative play was difficult to defend.*

*We put all our energy into defending which made it difficult to then put our energy into the attacks."*

-Marcelo Bielsa

Just before the season's second international break, United once again headed for South London, this time to face their old enemies Millwall, who had just witnessed the surprise resignation of manager and all-time leading goalscorer Neil Harris.

In contrast with the Club's inability of controlling the unruly elements of their fan base, Millwall's owners run a tight ship financially and continuity of management is usually how they operate.

**Millwall 2-1 Leeds United**
5th October, 2019

*Millwall*
Bialkowski, Romeo, Hutchinson, Cooper, M Wallace, J Wallace, Leonard (Williams 28), Molumby, Ferguson, Thompson (Bodvarsson 80), Bradshaw.

*Leeds United*
Casilla, Ayling, Berardi, White, Alioski, Phillips (Roberts 76), Klich, Dallas, Costa (Douglas 45), Harrison, Bamford (Nketiah 62).

Attendance: 16,311    Referee: James Linington

Once again, United visited the capital and came home empty handed. It must be said that the circumstances were, to say the least, dubious but that is often the way of things in the Championship.

The Whites had settled into their usual dominant pattern and all seemed well. However, disaster struck in the sixteenth minute when Tom Bradshaw dived theatrically in front of Gaetano Berardi.

The referee not only pointed to the penalty spot, but showed a straight red card to the bemused defender, who protested that he hadn't even made contact. Subsequent investigation proved this to be correct and the Swiss defender was spared suspension. JED WALLACE (16) duly scored from the penalty that followed.

United's ten men struggled on. Jack Harrison was himself floored in the Millwall penalty area, but unsurprisingly nobody was penalised for this.

These two setbacks seemed to knock the wind out of United's sails and they struggled to find their shape. On the stroke of half time, BRADSHAW (45) scored the second leaving United with a massive hill to climb.

That should have been that, but the Whites returned to the action like a team possessed. Almost immediately after the break, ALIOSKI (46) slid a shot home and suddenly it was Millwall who were on the back foot.

For half an hour, United played as if it was themselves who had the extra man, but it was all in vain. Needless to say, Bielsa did not complain about the referee but he was clearly disappointed with the manner in which United lost.

**League Position: 5th**

*"The result should be different. Each time we lose, I find few logical reasons to justify it. For me it's always a shame to explain why we lost. I think that with ten men, we were better than them. Always, we are trying to explain why what we want doesn't happen. It impacts the tolerance of the people who are listening."*

-Marcelo Bielsa

# Chapter Five
## Biblical Bielsa

United's 100th birthday was marked by the unveiling of a plaque at the Salem Chapel in Hunslet (where the club was formed), plus several dinners in the Centenary Pavilion. True to form, Marcelo Bielsa turned up to the black-tie event in his trademark Leeds United track gear.

Anybody else dressed in this manner would have been refused admission, but he hardly raised an eyebrow when joining the photoshoots.

**Leeds United 1-0 Birmingham City**
19th October, 2019

*Leeds United*
Casilla, Ayling, White, Berardi, Phillips, Dallas, Alioski, Klich (Roberts 61), Costa (Douglas 84), Bamford (Nketiah 45), Harrison.

*Birmingham City*
Camp, Colin, Roberts, Dean, Pederson, Crowley (Maghoma 67), Bellingham (Gardner 76), Sunjic, Villalba, Gimenez, Jutkiewicz (Bailey 76).

Attendance: 35,731    Referee: Robert Jones

Marcelo Bielsa resisted the temptation to give Eddie Nketiah a place in the starting line up, despite overwhelming pressure from just about everybody.

The Whites started well and assumed their usual dominance in the first half. Alioski, Costa, Dallas and Bamford all came close, but United went into the break level with their opponents. Lee Camp and his defence appeared to be in their usual uncompromising mood against Leeds and despite the bright start, the game was difficult to call.

Predictably, Nketiah replaced Bamford in the second half. Although his contribution was limited, he does seem to generate excitement and anticipation amongst the fans.

He was upended just outside the penalty area and Alioski, who was enjoying a fine game sent the resultant free kick high and wide. As the game passed the hour mark, Jack Harrison dispossessed Maxime Colin and burst forward to deliver a killer pass into the box.

Local hero, PHILLIPS (65), smashed home a cracking shot to send the United fans wild. It was fitting that Kalvin was in the right position as Eddie Nketiah had strayed into an offside position.

The Whites defended their advantage doggedly and Kiko Casilla pulled off a couple of fine saves before the final whistle sounded, accompanied by a great cheer of relief from the anxious crowd.

*"It was a really important game for us to win. I am not happy with how we closed the game out. After we scored, we could have finished the match and we gave them the ball and let them control the chances.*

*We had one of the best first halves we have played. We started the second half with some doubt and after the goal we had three chances to finish the match and then little by little, we allowed the opponent to control the ball. When they have the ball, they will have chances to score.*

*Sometimes God puts things in the right place. Phillips is playing at Leeds and now he will stay in the history of the club for this goal. We were very focused on the match. The team showed that in every moment."*

-Marcelo Bielsa

## League Position: 2nd

Away games at Preston North End are very popular with Leeds United fans for a number of reasons: It's not too far away for most fans, the locals are friendly and a large ticket allocation is given.

But above all, the police engage with the fans in a way that is an example to every other force in the country. They adopt a humorous, but firm non-confrontational approach, which in my opinion is unique.

Although Deepdale remains on its original site, it has been completely redeveloped but has managed to retain a lot of the atmosphere that modern grounds often lack.

The Lilywhites had started the season well, especially at home where they were unbeaten in the Championship having scored eighteen goals, with only six conceded. It was clear that this was going to be a tough test for United.

**Preston North End 1-1 Leeds United**
22nd October, 2019

*Preston North End*
Rudd, Fisher, Bauer, Davies, Rafferty, Pearson, Browne, Potts, Johnson, Barkhuizen (Green 90), Nugent (Maguire 72).

*Leeds United*
Casilla, Ayling, White, Berardi (Roberts 77), Alioski, Phillips, Costa, Dallas, Klich, Harrison, Bamford (Nketiah 77).

Attendance: 18,275    Referee: Kevin Friend

Both North End and United came racing out of the blocks, with both sides coming close to scoring from early corners. United gradually took control and had the crowd gasping as they sprayed passes across the park, pinning North End back for much of the first half.

Wasteful finishing once again prevented them from taking the initiative in a one-sided game. Bamford was by far the worst offender and although he worked hard and found himself in scoring positions, he couldn't convert his efforts into goals.

It was a very frustrating first half for United and on the occasions that North End were able to get an attack away, you felt that they were capable of scoring.

The Whites started the second half well, but it was the same old story of missed opportunities. Perhaps out of their acute frustration, they were starting to miss passes and get caught in possession. It was in one such lapse that they allowed the home side to take the lead.

Alioski sent a pass straight to a Preston defender who played it over his head. Maguire then picked the ball up and sent a cross for BARKHUIZEN (74) to tap in.

The home fans were delighted and a bit surprised as well. As for the United faithful, it seemed to us as if our old ghosts had come back to haunt us again.

As the clock ran down, Bielsa introduced Nketiah and Roberts in place of Bamford and Berardi, with thirteen minutes remaining. Ten minutes later, Nketiah was brought down thirty yards away from the Preston goal.

Phillips smashed the resultant free kick into the wall, before the ball ricocheted to Harrison who sent a fine cross to the far post and the arriving NKETIAH (87) produced a lovely header beyond the clutching hands of Rudd.

In the dying seconds, Roberts was brought down in the area but the referee waved play on.

This was a well-earned point for United and once again, Eddie Nketiah was the man who found the back of the net at the crucial moment.

**League Position: 2nd**

*"Until they scored, the match had a direction that was difficult to change. After the Preston goal, we multiplied our efforts to score. After we managed to score, we could have won the match. But we cannot ignore the fact that after they scored, they had some chances to score again. Maybe they could have won the match.*

*Until they scored, the match was completely for us. In this period, until we drew the match, we could have received the second goal or we could have a draw as we did.*

*What is clear is that the opponent does not need to command the match to create danger. We dominated a lot, we commanded the game, we created a lot of danger but it is difficult for us to unbalance the match.*

*When the match ends in a draw, we had a lot of chances to score and it seemed difficult today to score. After they scored, we continued to attack and there were some chances.*

*Linking my job here in Leeds, we could write a book about these kinds of situations."*

-Marcelo Bielsa

As I walked away from the ground with a feeling of great relief, I heard groups of Preston fans discussing the match. Far from moaning about the late equaliser, they were saying things like:

"How did we manage to draw?"

"They should have murdered us!"

"What a steal!"

I couldn't imagine our fans reacting that way to a game where the opposition had grabbed a late equaliser. Nevertheless, it showed how United's dominance was once again unable to produce a positive result.

All I wanted to do was find a nice pub, get a pint and open the Sky app on my phone to savour Eddie's goal once again and check the other scores.

The first pub that you hit on Church Street is Ye Olde Blue Bell, and it is a very nice establishment.

Samuel Smith's ales from Tadcaster are served, the prices are amazingly low, the beer is good and all should have been well.

Samuel Smith's is Yorkshire's oldest brewery, founded in 1758 and remains within ownership of the family.

The boss is the eccentric and secretive Humphrey Smith, who rules his empire with an iron fist. Mr. Smith does not like smart phones, laptops or tablets and has banned their use in all of his pubs. One must feel sorry for his staff who have to attempt to enforce this rule, but enforce it they do!

A couple of weeks earlier, Mr Smith visited his newest pub; the Fox and Goose in Droitwich, Worcestershire. The pub had been open for seven weeks and was doing well. Mr Smith overheard a customer use the 'f' word. The customer was telling a joke and did not do it in an aggressive manner, but it was enough to send Mr. Smith into a rage.

He ordered all the customers to leave the pub, emptied the cash register and closed the pub down permanently. Not wanting to bring the wrath of Humphrey Smith down on myself, I sat outside at one of the picnic tables to watch the goals back on my phone.

It was the finest of looping headers from Eddie Nketiah and it looked just as good on screen as it did from behind the goal.

Next up was another tough looking match as United took the short trip down the M1 to meet Sheffield Wednesday. The Owls were being managed by our old friend and sometime protagonist, Garry Monk.

Wednesday occupied third place in the table, with just one point less than United and had only lost one game at home.

**Sheffield Wednesday 0-0 Leeds United**
26th October, 2019

*Sheffield Wednesday*
Westwood, Fox, Hutchinson, Iorfa, Palmer, Harris, Bannan, Pelupessy (Lee 84), Reach, Fletcher, Nuhiu (Forestieri 86).

*Leeds United*
Casilla, Ayling, White, Berardi, Dallas, Phillips, Klich, Alioski, Costa (Cooper 76), Bamford (Nketiah 45), Harrison.

Attendance: 27,516    Referee: Tim Robinson

Once again, Bielsa ignored the almost unbearable pressure to start Eddie Nketiah and some of the less tolerant of our fans were starting to mutter again.

It was rightly pointed out that although United's defence was sound, the forwards (particularly Bamford) were not taking advantage of the many good chances that were being presented to them.

It was a lunchtime kick off to accommodate both Sky and the South Yorkshire Police. Just to help matters along, the trams to and from Hillsborough were suspended for the day.

The game started quietly for a local derby, with both sets of fans probably subdued by the incessant rain.

On nineteen minutes, United felt that they should have had a penalty when Nuhiu felled Ben White, who had moved the ball to the by-line after going up for a corner.

The referee waved play on, but this happening seemed to galvanise United and they produced some of their best football between the incident and half time. A war of attrition continued in the middle of the park as well, between Kalvin Phillips and former Whites loanee Barry Bannan.

Just before half time, there was action in both penalty boxes as both goalkeepers produced fantastic saves. First, Kiko Casilla tipped a thunderous effort from Steven Fletcher over the bar. The shot was clearly heading for the top corner.

Before the stunned crowd had time to catch their breath, Kieron Westwood was performing similar heroics at the other end. How he managed to get down to Patrick Bamford's cleverly placed header, only he will know. But it was enough to frustrate the normally stoic Bamford.

Worse was to come for the big striker, as he was replaced by Eddie Nketiah before the start of the second half.

Phillips came close before Fletcher smashed the ball against the crossbar, from where it hit an uncomprehending Kiko Casilla and bounced to safety. Nketiah was lucky not to be penalised as he caught Pelupessy with a swinging arm and the Owls were incensed as the referee allowed play to continue, as their man was nursing a head injury.

The Arsenal loanee was involved in United's best move of the second half, when he used his pace to get behind the Wednesday defence. He then pulled the ball back for Harrison, whose shot was blocked. Later on, Phillips sent in a good cross from the right which Alioski headed against the crossbar.

As the clock ran down, it became clear that this game was going to end goalless to the moans of a lot of fans. Not too long ago, both this game and the Preston match would have been seen as hard fought away draws against two teams with extremely good records at home.

However, since getting a taste of 'Bielsaball', what was served up here did nothing to stimulate jaded palates.

**League Position: 3rd**

"*It was a different match to the match we are used to playing. In the first half we played better but even when we controlled the match, they had chances.*

*In the second half it changed, sometimes we commanded it, sometimes they controlled it. We missed goals, they missed goals as well.*

*They in the second half could impose their style on ours for some moments. To analyse the match, we must give value to that. Also, how we built our chances established little difference for us in the game. One feature of the first half was that we had good opportunity and we had a lot of advantage, but we couldn't transform these situations in one chance.*

*The opponent had some good individual performances in the second half – Adam Reach, Kadeem Harris and Barry Bannan. When three attacking players improve their performance, the match changes. After we can say that it was a similar match for both teams because they had more chances but less clear than ours.*

*Bamford, he finished very well the last ball. The ball came from one side, he headed from the same side. Bamford is a player who has the ability, the skill to fight in the physical challenge.*

*Until today, we thought Eddie had less skill in this sense but today, he showed the opposite. Bamford is a player who knows how to mix the movement when he drops and goes deep again.*

*Today, Eddie showed he also can dribble in the one-on-ones, a skill that maybe Patrick uses less. Both are similar, I thought that in the second half, Nketiah was going to find the same match that Bamford found in the first half.*

*I thought that with our team close to their box, Nketiah would give us something more because when he arrives in the box, he does this with a lot of surprise. We realise when Pat is in the box, but Nketiah appears suddenly. After we played the match further from the box, Eddie adapted himself very well to this situation as well.*

*I saw a lot of good things today in Eddie, I didn't see that before in the performances. I give value to the spirit to compete, to recover the ball, to help the team pass through difficult moments and one great skill to unbalance the one-on-ones."*

-Marcelo Bielsa

The next game was Queens Park Rangers at home. More often than not, I attend this fixture and the one at Loftus Road with my old friend, Mike, who is a dyed in the wool Hoops fan.

On this occasion, we decided to stay in Leeds and have a night out after the match. In recent years, it has not been necessary for me to stay in town on a Saturday as I can usually get home after the match.

The only time I have used a hotel in recent years has been midweek, when I have used the excellent value Discovery Inn right opposite the railway station. I have paid as little as £35 for a night's stay, but no chance on a Saturday though.

Thanks to the modern miracle of 'dynamic pricing' a single room could not be acquired for less than £135 each. The story was much the same throughout the city centre, with budget chains even charging £120 on average.

This called for some innovative thinking to get the price down and to stay in the luxury that we have come to be accustomed with.

Although I was born in Beeston, I am no stranger to North Leeds having moved to Chapeltown at the age of eight. I was also educated at St. Michael's College in the Hyde Park area.

At £61 for a single room including breakfast, Hinsley Hall at Headingley seemed to be a very good option.

When we arrived, we found that it was a place for religious retreat owned by the Catholic Diocese of Leeds. Meeting rooms were dedicated to St. Hilda, Blessed Margaret Clitheroe and other saints with Yorkshire connections. This was not the sort of venue normally frequented by football fans, but it seemed peaceful and the reception staff were friendly and welcoming.

That very afternoon there was a talk on bereavement and spirituality. This would have been very useful for me to attend after the play off defeat to Derby, but all was positive in this new season and so we decided to go to the match instead.

The rooms were absolutely fine and the dining room was adequate. The bar looked like a bit of an afterthought, but you can't have everything in life.

Bielsa had hinted before the game that Eddie Nketiah had finally done enough to start against Queens Park Rangers. He had not indicated as to whether this would be in place of Patrick Bamford or alongside him.

Unfortunately, Nketiah had picked up an abdominal injury in training on the Friday and would not be available for selection. There was some good news however, because Tyler Roberts started and Pablo Hernandez was named as a substitute after a long absence.

**Leeds United 2-0 Queens Park Rangers**
2nd November, 2019

*Leeds United*
Casilla, Ayling, White, Cooper, Dallas, Phillips, Klich, Costa (Hernandez 77), Roberts, Harrison (Davis 83), Bamford.

*Queens Park Rangers*
Kelly, Rangel, Hall, Leistner (Kane 54), Wallace, Manning, Chair (Pugh 63), Ball, Eze, Wells (Mlakar 72), Hugill.

Attendance: 35,284    Referee: Geoff Eltringham

Unlike many teams this season, Rangers came to Elland Road to attack. This was when United allowed them to, which wasn't very often.

Taking 51% of the possession, the Hoops showed why they have scored so many goals. Nevertheless, United came out on top on every other meaningful statistic and peppered the Rangers goal repeatedly.

The visitors also demonstrated why they have shipped so many goals, as their nervy defence struggled to contain United's offensive force. Bielsa had decided to play with three players across the back in Ayling, Cooper and White.

This was designed to nullify Rangers' bold attacking strategy and allow Stuart Dallas to man-mark the phenomenally talented Eberechi Eze.

Bamford, Klich and Harrison all missed golden opportunities to score before Jack Harrison cut the ball back from the touchline and ROBERTS (39) gratefully pounced on the ball, smashing it into the back of the net.

For the remainder of the first half, there was some good football from both sides along with some scrappy stuff, mostly in front of the John Charles Stand. Just before half time, Jordan Hugill came very close to equalising in front of the Kop as he slid towards the ball which just eluded him.

The second half saw United hammering away and Bamford was extremely unlucky to have a fine diving header adjudged to be offside by the narrowest of margins.

Pablo Hernandez played a little cameo role in the dying minutes, replacing Costa. The little Spaniard showed some nice touches and was enthusiastically received after his extended absence.

Justice was finally done in the last ten minutes when HARRISON (83) played the ball off a Hoops defender, picked it up again and coolly steered the ball into the net. The cheer that went up was tinged with relief as it was clear that the game was now beyond the Londoners.

**League Position: 1st**

*"We were calm and if we win by one goal and you have five minutes left then everybody is nervous in the stadium. So, we hope that match to match, we don't have any more of this feeling. And we try to pass this kind of match where we are winning 1-0 more relaxed."*

-Marcelo Bielsa

It was good to have time for a couple of pints after the match and so we headed straight to the Old White Hart in Beeston to await the dispersal of the crowds. Later, we repaired to The Hop before having a curry at the Shabab which has been a favourite eating place for more years than I care to remember.

We decided to finish the evening in Headingley and though impressed by other elements of the Hinsley Hall operation, we felt that the bar might not be the sort of place where you could refresh the body as well as the soul.

This meant a trip to the Original Oak, where I had worked as a part-time barman more than fifty years ago. In those days, the choice was mild, bitter or lager. I'm not sure why we opted to finish the evening on the potent Chieftain IPA from Franciscan Wells in Cork, but this was the choice.

Maybe it was the religious sounding name of it which was in keeping with our nearby hotel. Who knows? The Lord moves in mysterious ways.

In any event, it was not a wise choice as this comforting, treacle-like beer went down far too easily.

However, on the night itself oblivion was achieved almost immediately. Another plus point of Hinsley Hall is that it's not the sort of place where your fellow guests go running up and down the corridors, banging on your room door and screaming obscenities!

Back at reception, I saw a sign which read: 'Those bearing witness to the Canonisation of Blessed Marcelo Bielsa, please report to the Margaret Clitherow Room.'

To sate my curiosity, I walked down the corridor towards the room in question. Outside the room was a queue of athletic looking young men. They were all soberly dressed with the exception of one strange fellow with bleached blonde hair.

He was dressed in full clown attire while running up and down the queue trying to make his colleagues laugh. He then started singing in a toneless voice:

"Don't you know pump it up, the Whites are going up, don't you know pump it up." He repeated the chorus over and over again like a bored child.

"That's enough now Gjanni, this is supposed to be a serious occasion." Said a tall man who seemed to have an air of authority about him.

"Please Liam, just one more somersault, and that's it. I promise." Gjanni replied.

The first young man to enter the Margaret Clitherow room was a muscular guy with an extravagant hairstyle.

Incredibly, Pope Francis was sat at the far end of the room on a raised seat. He was dressed all in white, which I took as a good omen.

"What is your name, young man?"

"Kalvin, your Holiness."

"Come forth and bear witness." The Pope said, sounding strangely like Vic Reeves.

"I was a young midfielder, learning my trade when in less than a year Blessed Marcelo developed me into a top player with international prospects…"

One by one, the young men entered the room and told of the miracles wrought by Blessed Marcelo and how he had transformed their mundane careers, turning them into stars. Suddenly, there was a familiar sound which became louder and louder until I reached for the snooze button on my phone.

I awoke to the reality of a cold Yorkshire morning with a nasty hangover, but with the nice, warm feeling that the gathering of three more points always brings. No more Chieftain IPA for me.

Nevertheless, a good cooked breakfast was enjoyed later and I was very proud of myself keeping the banter to a minimum.

This is an arrangement that Mike and I have had for many years and came in particularly useful last February when Rangers robbed us of our game in hand. As we all know, this prefaced more than two months of nervous nail biting leading to the ultimate disappointment against Derby.

# Chapter Six
## Notable November

Twenty-four hours before the victory against Queens Park Rangers, a rather striking centenary tribute was unveiled in the southern part of the city.

The footbridge for the M621 is usually a quiet area of Leeds throughout the week, but on match days there will be hundreds of people who pass by on their way to Elland Road. Because of this, artist and lifelong United supporter Shane Green wanted to give something back to his fellow supporters.

On either side of a prominent crest, there are several diagonal yellow lines which Green says represents the club going onwards and upwards.

Shane Green's mural on a house in Tilbury Mount, Holbeck.

**Leeds United 2-1 Blackburn Rovers**
9th November, 2019

*Leeds United*
Casilla, Ayling, White, Cooper (Berardi 72), Dallas, Phillips, Costa (Hernandez 81), Klich, Roberts, Harrison (Davis 90), Bamford.

*Blackburn Rovers*
Walton, Bennett, Nyambe, Adarabioyo, Williams, Travis, Holtby (Evans 69), Armstrong (Graham 60), Dack, Downing, Gallagher (Buckley 69).

Attendance: 35,567    Referee: Gavin Ward

Another near-capacity crowd saw United do the business against a very ordinary Blackburn side. The Whites began in their usual barnstorming manner, pinning Rovers back at every opportunity and a breakthrough came after half an hour.

Ayling stormed into the penalty area only to be upended.  But who would take the penalty? The fans held their breath when Patrick Bamford stepped forward. This was an act of considerable courage by the big striker who was clearly determined to bring his goal drought to an end.

BAMFORD (30) made no mistake and the relief around the ground was palpable.

The goal clearly inspired the hard-working striker to send an inch perfect pass to (HARRISON 35), who scored off the inside of the post. Both players had repaid faith shown in them by Marcelo Bielsa.

At this point of the proceedings, it felt like there was going to be a feast of goals but it wasn't to be. The visitors even scored a goal of their own before half time, when WILLIAMS (40) rose above Ayling to head past Casilla.

This came as a result of a corner which says more about opponents being unable to score very often from open play against United than the Whites' vulnerability at set pieces.

Harrison came closest in a second half which was dominated by a midfield battle between Kalvin Phillips and Bradley Dack.

Worryingly, Cooper hobbled off late in the game, being replaced by the ever-reliable Gaetano Berardi.

Whilst a more emphatic win would have been welcome, United are starting to develop a very solid, uncompromising look ahead of yet another international break.

**League Position: 3rd**

*"Bamford is a player with a big character and a big personality. He took the responsibility for the penalty which isn't easy for him.*

*At that moment it was difficult to think that the opponent could score but after they scored, everything changed. After we scored twice, we had ten or twelve chances but in the first and second half we had a lot of spaces to attack. We didn't take advantage of that as much as we should have."*

-Marcelo Bielsa

One of the dafter happenings during the latest international break was when a member of the Bedfordshire Constabulary issued a tweet saying that he was pleased to oversee the policing for 'this important match with two great sets of fans.'

Unfortunately, he accompanied the tweet with a stock photo of the boys in blue in full riot gear complete with shields and batons.

From memory, the last time I saw police in riot gear at a Leeds game was back in 1990 at Bournemouth. This was when United won promotion from the old Second Division almost thirty years ago.

When this fact was pointed out to the officer, he tried to justify it several times before realising that he was fighting a losing battle and apologising.

As things stand in the Championship, Luton is the nearest ground to where I live and so I was determined to get a ticket even though they were in very short supply.

Even I would have difficulty explaining to my wife that I was off to Elland Road to attend a beamback of a game that was taking place ten miles up the road!

Having acquired a ticket in the home end from a good friend and Luton resident, I hopped on the train to travel the ten minute journey to this most depressing of Bedfordshire towns.

I walked out of the station and up to the Painters Arms for a couple of pints of Guinness. I had done some business a couple of years ago with the former landlord; Gerry from Derry, but I learned that he had been gone for a while.

I sat in the corner and settled down to watch the West Ham versus Spurs match on the television. Before long some Leeds fans arrived. Like myself, they were not wearing colours and before very long a good conversation was being had with some Luton Town fans. It was all very good natured and well behaved.

Just then, two police officers arrived, the 'guardians of peace' introduced themselves to the bar staff and then proceeded to fine tune their ears in order to pick up any alien accents.

"Are you lads from Leeds?" They were heard to enquire.

"We are." Replied one of the United fans.

"It's just that most of your lads are drinking down in the town." Responded one of the officers with a degree of tact not shown previously by his boss.

Sensibly, the lads did not react to this and when it was clear that they were not going to leave the pub, the police decided to return to their van and look for trouble elsewhere.

I repaired to the Shahi Grill on Dunstable Road for an excellent Lamb Tikka rolled in a Nan Bread which took so long to serve that I had to ask them to wrap it up for me so I could take it to the match.

**Luton Town 1-2 Leeds United**
23rd November, 2019

*Luton Town*
Shea, Bree, Bradley, Collins, Potts, Pearson, Mpanzu, Shinnie (Bolton 90), Tunnicliffe, Brown (LuaLua 75), Cornick (McManaman 75).

*Leeds United*
Casilla, Ayling, White, Berardi (Cooper 59), Dallas, Phillips, Hernandez, Klich, Roberts (Clarke 71), Harrison (Costa 64), Bamford.

Attendance: 10,068    Referee: John Brooks

United started brightly and both Tyler Roberts and Patrick Bamford came close to scoring. For Luton, former United 'lost boy' Izzy Brown caught the eye with his towering presence.

He really does look like a class act and Luton are lucky to have him in their side. The other Luton player who stood out was goalkeeper James Shea. Shea appeared to be having the game of his life as keepers tend to do when their team plays Leeds.

Early in the second half, Kalvin Phillips managed to dispossess Brown. The 'Yorkshire Pirlo' was as tigerish as ever and while Brown and his teammates were calling for a foul, the city's favourite son slipped the ball to Ben White who sent BAMFORD (51) away to make a cool and well taken finish.

United continued to press but were startled by a quick equaliser when COLLINS (54) powered home a header, totally against the run of play.

Emboldened by this, the Luton faithful forgot themselves briefly and started to make a noise.

Nevertheless, the Whites took control again and Mateusz Klich sent a killer assist into the Luton box. Both Patrick Bamford and PEARSON (90) scrambled for it and the Luton defender was credited with turning it into his own net.

This was a tough, hard fought match and United will be both happy and relieved to head north with the three points.

**League Position: 2nd**

*"You play in small sized spaces. When you have reduced sized spaces it's always difficult for the team who attacks and with the pitch smaller, this difficulty increases. That means that the defending team can counter attack.*

*This is a team very compact in defence, they recover and they counter attack very fast. They play long balls after to recover. In this pitch, long balls mean going from box to box.*

*I think the result was fair. A good performance from the team. In the first half it was a little easier but in the second half, we fought a little bit more. Usually it's very difficult to win."*

-Marcelo Bielsa

**Reading 0-1 Leeds United**
26th November, 2019

*Reading*
Cabral, Gunter, Miazga, Morrison, Moore, Richards, Swift, Rinomhota (McCleary 90), Ejaria, Meite (Loader 86), Puscas (Boye 70).

*Leeds United*
Casilla, Ayling, White, Cooper, Dallas, Phillips, Klich (Alioski 66), Hernandez, Roberts (Costa 35), Harrison (Shackleton 90), Bamford.

Attendance: 16,918    Referee: Darren Bond

If the Luton Town game was a struggle against a team that would have been perfectly happy with one point, then this was similar. In addition to this, Reading managed to serve up some of the most negative football that we have seen this season.

Tyler Roberts had to hobble off after only thirty-five minutes and was replaced by Helder Costa.

Although there were plenty of corners, shots on goal were at a premium for both sides. Stuart Dallas came closest just after the hour, rattling the Reading crossbar with a finely struck volley.

When the goal finally came, it was a thing of beauty. Swift shot a free kick for the Royals from a long way out, but Casilla was on hand to beat it away as far as Alioski.

The North Macedonian then made good ground before finding Costa who sent a perfect cross to the far post. HARRISON (86) made no mistake with a fine header.

United took no chances in the remaining minutes and once again showed that they had the ability to wear down an inferior side with their superior skill and fitness.

**League Position: 1st**

*"When you are top of the league, it is better than the other positions in the table. But it is also true that today, it does not mean a lot. The most important thing is what happens in May.*

*Tonight, was a tight match, it was difficult for us to create danger in the first half. In the second half, we changed and we attacked a little more. And enough to deserve the win. We defended well when we had to. Reading's chances were linked only to set pieces. It was a very demanding match but we were able to stay without conceding a goal. We had patience.*

*This is a signal of the maturity and experience of the team. It showed in the way that we managed the ball, especially in the centre of the pitch."*

-Marcelo Bielsa

**Leeds United 4-0 Middlesbrough**
30th November, 2019

*Leeds United*
Casilla, Ayling, White, Cooper, Dallas, Phillips (Berardi 83), Klich, Costa (Alioski 76), Hernandez, Harrison, Bamford (Nketiah 79).

*Middlesbrough*
Pears, Bola, McNair, Ayala, Fry, Howson, Wing (Liddle 70), Tavernier, Saville, Fletcher (Walker 90), Assombalonga (O'Neill 77).

Attendance: 35,626    Referee: Keith Stroud

After a series of hard-fought wins by narrow margins, it was good to enjoy a convincing and well-deserved win at Elland Road. BAMFORD (3) opened the proceedings with a diving header as a result of a signature pinpoint cross from Hernandez.

The big striker was in action again just before the break, providing a lovely lay off for KLICH (45+3) to slot home.

Middlesbrough had not been in the contest and for once it seemed that United were going to win by a comfortable margin.

Throughout the second half, United never took their foot off the gas pedal. COSTA (67) was next to score as he finally opened his Championship account for United. He weaved his way single handedly through the Boro defence to smash home a well-deserved goal.

KLICH (73) put the icing on to the cake with a real screamer. This brought back memories of his series of long-range strikes during the first part of the previous season.

Perhaps the most impressive part of this performance was the way that Leeds never let up as they ruthlessly tore Boro apart. Indeed, Stuart Dallas and Gjanni Alioski were both making gut-busting runs even as the final whistle was blown.

**League Position: 1st**

*"We defended very well. There was a moment in the first half when Middlesbrough created a lot of chances. It's important, we have to say they missed eight senior players through injury. They lost an impact. The players they missed are proper players and if they had all of their players, then maybe the match would have been more difficult."*

-Marcelo Bielsa

**Huddersfield Town 0-2 Leeds United**
7th December, 2019

*Huddersfield Town*
Grabara, Duhaney, Schindler, Stankovic, Hadergjonaj, Kachunga, Hogg, Bacuna, Karoma (Harratt 72), Grant, Mounie (Daly 83).

*Leeds United*
Casilla, Ayling, White, Berardi, Dallas, Klich (Casey 85), Alioski, Costa (Douglas 87), Hernandez, Harrison, Bamford (Nketiah 77).

Attendance: 23,805    Referee: Gavin Ward

For the first forty-five minutes, the Terriers lived up to their name. Not only did they bag 50% of the possession but they came very close to scoring. Their side was depleted and they started with just three substitutes on the bench.

Nevertheless, they were in no mood to step aside and allow United to bulldoze their way through.

Ben White had been moved forward to play the holding role in the place of the suspended Kalvin Phillips and it must be said that the Brighton loanee looked less than comfortable in this role.

Kiko Casilla showed his class on several occasions including making a fine save from Steve Mounie and Luke Ayling headed a powerful shot away from Karlan Grant.

At the other end, Klich rattled the crossbar with a rasping effort which was the closest that United came to breaching the Town defence.

The second half was five minutes old when Pablo Hernandez sent in a lovely corner which was cleared as far as the edge of the penalty area. ALOSKI (50) was waiting to pounce and smashed a great volley through the crowded box.

On 77 minutes, Eddie Nketiah replaced Patrick Bamford, who once again left the field to rapturous applause from the Leeds fans. He had worked his heart out in all areas of the pitch and had taken the time to wind the Huddersfield players up both on and off the ball. He seems to be really relishing his role of pantomime villain.

Nketiah was to play his part in United's final goal. It was a lovely team effort that started on the right side of the Leeds defence, picked up by Nketiah in the middle of the park. The Arsenal loanee sent Jack Harrison haring down the left wing.

The Manchester City loanee then sent a perfect cross for HERNANDEZ (78) to nod home at the far post. In fairness to Town, they kept on trying and given a bit better luck could have caused a problem.

*"In the first half, we should have created more chances. We had some opportunities to have a chance but we couldn't end it very well.*
*In all the match but especially the second half, we defended the set pieces badly.*

*Our first goal from Alioski made it easier for us to develop the play in the second half. We could have scored more goals but we could have received one goal as well. By January, Huddersfield will be a side that is on the way up."*

-Marcelo Bielsa

**Leeds United 2-0 Hull City**
10th December, 2019

*Leeds United*
Casilla, Ayling, White, Berardi, Dallas, Phillips, Costa (Struijk 90), Hernandez, Klich (Douglas 90), Harrison (Alioski 69), Bamford.

*Hull City*
Long, Lichaj, Burke, De Wijs, Elder (Lewis-Porter 85), Bowen, Batty (Bowler 74), Lopes, Grosicki (Honeyman 90), Irvine, Eaves.

Attendance: 35,200    Referee: David Webb

This ended up being United's seventh win in a row and was typical of the solid performances, often clean sheets which had graced November and early December. The Whites dominated the first half and played some scintillating football but could not convert this into goals.

As usual, they had the lion's share of the possession and on the occasions when they lost possession, they won it back very quickly. By contrast, United were not nearly as impressive in the second half but their persistence finally paid dividends.

Helder Costa was having a good game and when he whipped a killer cross into the Hull City box, DE WIJS (73) could only turn the ball into his own net to United's delight and Hull's heartbreak.

At the other end, Tom Eaves broke free and headed the ball towards goal. Casilla saved and immediately initiated a counter attack. In an instant, the ball was at the other end of the pitch.

Mateusz Klich pulled the ball back for Patrick Bamford who struck the post with his effort. Thankfully, ALIOSKI (83) was alert and netted from the rebound. The North Macedonian later sent another fine cross to Patrick Bamford who was unlucky not to score himself.

Yet again, United's tenacity and superior fitness saw them through towards the end of a game. Not pretty stuff, but another valuable three point haul.

**League Position: 1st**

*"Two different halves. Our first half was very good. We faced an opponent that has a very attractive style with attackers. Midfielders that want to play. A team with full backs who make important attacks. In the first half, we were superior to them.*

*In the second half, they balanced the match, the match was more for both sides. They have had chances; elaborate chances and we couldn't stop them. We kept the offensive but it was more difficult to defend than in the first half.*

*After we scored the first goal, we started to manage the game better but there were moments when we risked the result."*

-Marcelo Bielsa

# Chapter Seven
## Seasonal Stumble

Four days later, Cardiff City were the visitors to Elland Road. They had recently appointed former Millwall boss Neil Harris as their manager after parting company with Neil Warnock.

Warnock was reportedly looking for 'one last challenge' before retirement and has been trotting out this message for several years now. It will be no surprise if he appears elsewhere before very long.

**Leeds United 3-3 Cardiff City**
14th December, 2019

*Leeds United*
Casilla, Ayling, White, Berardi (Struijk 84), Dallas, Phillips, Costa, Hernandez, Klich, Harrison (Alioski 81), Bamford (Nketiah 77).

*Cardiff City*
Etheridge, Peltier, Flint (Nelson 41), Morrison, Bennett, Mendez-Laing, Vaulks (Whyte 61), Pack, Ralls, Ward (Glatzel 73), Tomlin.

Attendance: 34,552    Referee: Tony Harrington

Prior to this game, United had gone on a ten match unbeaten run, scoring thirteen goals and only conceding three. The defensive solidity was a talking point throughout the league and it seemed almost churlish to mention that they could have scored a few more on the way.

This minor niggle seemed to have been put to bed when United stormed into a three goal lead, playing the best and most dominant football that we had witnessed all season.

The first goal was beautiful to behold and once again came from a lightning break. After a Cardiff corner, Harrison picked the ball up and raced up field, squaring the ball to Pablo Hernandez. The Spaniard then sent a pinpoint pass to COSTA (6) who relished the easy task of slotting the ball home.

Two minutes later, the home crowd were in heaven as Jack Harrison found Stuart Dallas who in turn set up BAMFORD (8) at the far post. The big striker had time to chest the ball down before lashing it into the back of the net.

After having a convincing penalty claim denied when Costa was scythed down, the Whites left the pitch at half time to tumultuous applause.

Early in the second half, Cardiff keeper, Neil Etheridge was judged to have brought Patrick Bamford down in the penalty area. BAMFORD (52) made no mistake with the resulting spot kick.

Then disaster struck. Casilla failed to properly clear a cross and old adversary TOMLIN (60) took advantage to pull one back for Cardiff and open the door to the madness which was to follow.

United held firm for another twenty-two minutes, but MORRISON (82) stooped to nod a cross home. The same player was sent off for fouling Eddie Nketiah shortly afterwards, but this didn't slow Cardiff's momentum. Tomlin back-heeled a long ball to GLATZEL (88) who levelled the scores.

United stormed forward and should have grabbed a late winner with both Nketiah and White coming very close as the clock ran down.

**League Position: 2nd**

*"Obviously, we cannot explain the result but it wasn't how we controlled the match that allowed us to think that we would draw the match. We played the same way at 3-1, 3-2 and 3-3.*

*When we were 3-3, we had two chances to win the match, we cannot explain it. In this match, we cannot explain this because of how we controlled the match. In other matches, we didn't manage them well. How we managed other matches justified their creating danger but, in this match, that didn't happen but we are responsible for this because we cannot explain the result."*

-Marcelo Bielsa

The last game before Christmas was away to Fulham. For this to take place on a Saturday was a rarity, as the last few encounters had been night matches, presumably to protect the good citizens of SW6 from the northern hordes.

This season, Craven Cottage was being redeveloped which cut the capacity. This along with it being a Saturday put further pressure on the availability of tickets and I was unable to find one from my usual sources. This ended up with me finding a seat at the Fulham end, which was better than nothing.

Coming out of Putney Bridge station, I passed the Eight Bells pub which was packed solid with United fans. Nothing wrong with that, but I didn't fancy waiting fifteen minutes for a pint.

Instead, I went into the King's Arms which is situated a bit further down New King's Road. Another attraction of this pub was the excellent pint I had, which came all the way from Wiltshire.

Founded in 1875, Wadworth & Co's brewery is situated in the small market town of Devizes and is best known for the production of its 6X original ale. Having said that, the King's Arms is the only pub in London (and almost the rest of the country) serving Wadworth's 4.1% signature beer outside the south west. It certainly went down a treat!

Of course, there were plenty of Leeds fans around in the pub as well and I struck up a conversation with a couple of them. One man looked vaguely familiar and after expanding the conversation, I realised that I did not know him at all.

However, I did know his father quite well. Don Deedigan was a contemporary and friend of my own father in the Irish pub scene in Leeds many years ago. Don ran many successful pubs, most notably 'The Scott Hall' which was a great music venue and became synonymous with Northern Soul.

I had a great chat about old times with Don junior and his friend Martyn, while enjoying a few pints and some pizza before heading off to the match.

I took my place in good time before the game started and noticed a strange object on my seat. The object in question was a 'clapper', which if shaken vigorously produces a snapping sound. As a boy, I was an avid reader of comics. For some reason, usually in the autumn, rival publications used to come complete with free gifts.

Most boys will also remember League Ladders. Tiny pieces of cardboard were slotted into the ladders to indicate your position in the league. Before the season started, I always placed Leeds on top but usually lost interest towards the end of September as reality struck.

But here we were in 2019 as adults being asked to wave these things about to create 'atmosphere'.

**Fulham 2-1 Leeds United**
21st December, 2019

*Fulham*
Rodak, Christie, Mawson, Ream, Bryan, Cairney, Reed (Johansen 90), Onomah, Cavaleiro (Knockaert 90), Mitrovic, Decordova-Reid (Sessegnon 90).

*Leeds United*
Casilla, Ayling (Stevens 72), White, Cooper, Dallas, Phillips, Costa (Nketiah 45), Klich, Hernandez (Alioski 3), Harrison, Bamford.

Attendance: 18,878    Referee: Tim Robinson

In the recent past, United fans could console themselves with defeat when one of their 'bogey' teams beat them. However, with the arrival of Marcelo Bielsa, a lot of these traumas were discarded and the goblins were seen running back to their caves.

Unfortunately, Fulham did not fall into that category and hearing their fans singing 'Leeds are falling apart' would offend the ears of any decent fan. Leeds did not fall apart, they put up a pretty good fight and were extremely unlucky not to take at least one point.

After three minutes, Pablo Hernandez pulled up with a hamstring injury. He was replaced by Gjanni Alioski, which set the scene for what was to come.

Fulham were awarded a penalty when Ben White was adjudged to have fouled Bobby Decordova-Reid, who made a spectacular dive before writhing in agony. When this was played back, it was obvious that there was very minimal contact.

The injustice was made complete when MITROVIC (7) slid the ball past Kiko Casilla. The Spaniard pushed the ball on to the inside of the post but the ball trickled in to give Fulham the lead.

The first half continued as an end to end battle with Mateusz Klich grazing the post with a fine effort.

After half time, Eddie Nketiah replaced the ineffective Helder Costa and the Arsenal loanee was heavily involved in United's goal. Alioski sent a teasing ball through to Nketiah, who smashed it goal bound.

The shot was too hot for Rodak to handle and he was only able to parry it to BAMFORD (54), who had the simple task of slotting it in.

Leeds then started to dominate. Alioski came close with a header after good work from Nketiah and Harrison. Slowly but surely though, Fulham worked their way back into the game. Cavaleiro unleashed a mighty shot which Casilla tipped over the bar.

Shortly afterwards, White failed to clear the ball fully from the menacing Mitrovic. ONOMAH (69) then latched on to it and smashed an unstoppable shot into the United net.

Alioski, Klich and Nketiah were all involved in frantic action as the minutes ticked away. But it was to no avail and the Whites left Craven Cottage with only one win in the last eighteen visits to London.

**League Position: 2nd**

*"We played against one of the more powerful opponents. We defended well, they scored from one corner and one penalty.*

*They had just one more chance, whilst we had seven or eight chances to win the match. We defended very well because we play against great attackers.*

*Honestly, I don't want to not give value to what the opponent did but I did not see the opponent's attackers unbalance the game. We are talking about Cavaleiro and Mitrovic, they are maybe the most important in the league. It's clear Fulham are the best team in the Championship, but today the things they created; they could not score with."*

-Marcelo Bielsa

United were back in action at Elland Road on Boxing Day against Preston North End, which marked the beginning of the season's second half.

**Leeds United 1-1 Preston North End**
26th December, 2019

*Leeds United*
Casilla, Ayling, White, Cooper, Alioski, Phillips,
Costa, Dallas, Klich, Harrison, Bamford (Nketiah
64).

*Preston North End*
Rudd, Clarke, Huntington, Davies, Hughes,
Pearson, Browne, Maguire (Stockley 90+4), Potts,
Barkhuizen (Harrop 90), Nugent (Ledson 69).

Attendance: 35,638    Referee: Darren Bond

United seemed to struggle to get started and we
witnessed the spectacle of the Whites being pinned
back by their opponents early in the game.

Bamford had a shot deflected and although United
started to gain possession, their build up was
ponderous and they were caught napping too many
times. Casilla went walkabout and completely
mistimed a sliding tackle. To the relief of the home
crowd, Brad Potts mercifully missed the welcoming
empty net.

Later, Dallas shot down the middle and released the
ball to Klich, who dwelled too long on the ball
allowing Preston to give the Whites a dose of their
own medicine. North End countered swiftly and
sent (BROWNE 22) through to beat Casilla easily.

This warning did not wake United up immediately but towards the end of the first half, Alioski came close and Ayling was unlucky with an effort from twenty yards, as well as a header.

Bielsa made no changes at half time and Preston came out with the avowed intention to 'park the bus'. This led to a succession of niggly fouls and the referee seemed to be on the verge of losing control of the match altogether.

Just after the hour mark, Eddie Nketiah replaced Patrick Bamford and while the fans were happy enough to see the Arsenal loanee, the removal of Bamford was not a popular move.

Nketiah was unlucky to see his header pushed around the post by Rudd as the Whites continued to press. With very little time remaining, United's 'never say die' spirit paid off with (DALLAS 89) scoring with the help of a deflection.

**League Position: 2nd**

*"I was not happy with the first twenty minutes, it was not a good spell for us, we did not cope with the pressing and did not get into our game. I felt we took control after their goal. It was a better display from then and we controlled 75% of the game. We had enough chances to win the game towards the end and we probably should have won it. I admire Preston for how they got at us in the first quarter of the game.*

*They worked very hard to put us under pressure and close us down. We struggled to move the ball today. We had to move it sideways a lot and when we lost the ball going across the line it created problems for ourselves. I think we pressed the self-destruct button a few times which gave Preston their chances."*

-Marcelo Bielsa

The last game of 2019 and in fact the decade, was away at Birmingham City, which wasn't a happy place for United in recent seasons. This was another game that I had difficulty finding tickets for and so, I found myself seated amongst the Peaky Blinders. As events would subsequently prove, it was not the best game to hide your emotions!

## Birmingham City 4-5 Leeds United
29th December, 2019

*Birmingham City*
Trueman, Colin, Dean, Harding, Pedersen, Bellingham (Montero 74), Sunjic, Gardner, Crowley (Bela 68), Mrabti (Gimenez 74), Jutkiewicz.

*Leeds United*
Casilla, Ayling, White, Cooper, Dallas, Phillips, Alioski, Costa, Klich (Berardi 86), Harrison, Nketiah (Roberts 81).

Attendance: 22,059    Referee: Keith Stroud

The old proverb says 'don't get angry, get even'. In this game, Luke Ayling did both and more besides. With a game like this though, it is always best to start at the beginning. Leeds powered into a two goal lead in short order and it looked as though a massacre was going to follow.

Eddie Nketiah led the line as Patrick Bamford had picked up a slight knock. It felt like an ideal chance for the loanee to strut his stuff, as it was still unclear whether he would be staying in the New Year.

Once again, the opener came from a counter. Jack Harrison picked the ball up from a Birmingham corner and sped away with the ball. His pass let in COSTA (15), who raced into the Blues' penalty box and sent a fine shot across Trueman and into the net.

Six minutes later, Eddie Nketiah did some fine hold-up work, letting in Stuart Dallas, who found Gjanni Alioski who in turn squared it to HARRISON (21) who scored courtesy of a deflection. Some sloppy defending led to a Blues goal, neatly taken by BELLINGHAM (27).

This should have served as a warning to United but they played most of the remainder of the first half on the back foot. The sixteen-year-old Jude Bellingham seemed to be here, there and everywhere as United struggled to stay in front.

In the second half, Kalvin Phillips dropped back to bolster up the defence but just after the hour, United were made to pay for their lack of invention. Kiko Casilla failed to clear a corner and JUTKIEWICZ (61) headed home.

Luke Ayling was clearly not having any of this and he charged around the pitch like a madman. Alioski passed the ball to AYLING (69) on the right wing and the defender carried the ball to the edge of the penalty area, before volleying it into the net.

Only seven minutes of normal time were left when BELA (83) put City level for a third time.
A minute later, Ayling powered his way through the centre of the pitch, playing a quick exchange with Harrison. When he received the ball back, the ex-Bristol City man sent it through to DALLAS (84) who regained the lead for the Whites.

In the breathless twelve minutes that remained, JUTKIEWICZ (90+1) equalised for the fourth time before further madness. Ayling powered his way up the right touchline and sent in a defence-splitting cross, which the hapless HARDING (90+5) could only turn into his own net.

**League Position: 1st**

*"We had high efficiency to score, we are a team that need a lot of chances to score and we didn't have safety in defence. And we conceded goals that normally we would be in good condition to resolve.*

*We should have controlled the match more in the first half. It was difficult for us.*

*After the first part of the second half, the match had no definition even though we improved during this period and after the 2-2 the match was weird, strange. Every time Birmingham scored; we had the energy to go for one more goal."*

-Marcelo Bielsa

Along with this result at St. Andrew's, a few miles up the road, West Bromwich Albion suffered a shock home defeat at the hands of Middlesbrough.

This meant that the Whites would not only finish the year at the Championship summit, but the decade as well. The extraordinary statistic was then revealed that United have finished the last four decades at the top of their respective divisions.

| | | |
|---|---|---|
| *1989* | *Second Division* | *Tier 2* |
| *1999* | *Premier League* | *Tier 1* |
| *2009* | *League One* | *Tier 3* |
| *2019* | *Championship* | *Tier 2* |

This information gave great encouragement to the prophesiers, who already set about predicting the Whites' 2029-2030 fortunes.

Back to the 2019-2020 season and United at this stage were nine points clear of third place Fulham, heading into the new calendar year.

# Chapter Eight
## Joyless January

The new decade started with a visit to The Hawthorns and United's closest promotion rival, West Bromwich Albion.

The previous season, this match had produced United's heaviest defeat, when the Baggies came out 4-1 winners. Admittedly, the Whites had taken their revenge at Elland Road, scoring four themselves against Albion. Earlier in the current season, United had edged past their West Midlands rivals, 1-0.

**West Bromwich Albion 1-1 Leeds United**
1st January, 2020

*West Bromwich Albion*
Johnstone, Furlong, Ajayi, Bartley, Gibbs (Townsend 18), Livermore, Sawyers, Phillips (Zohore 84), Pereira, Krovinovic (Edwards 62), Robson-Kanu.

*Leeds United*
Casilla, Ayling, White, Cooper, Alioski (Douglas 45), Phillips, Costa, Klich, Dallas, Harrison, Nketiah (Bamford 45).

Attendance: 25,618    Referee: Robert Jones

West Brom started like a house on fire and went ahead inside two minutes. The Baggies were awarded a corner after good work from Matt Phillips. Casilla failed to properly clear the cross and AJAYI (2) poked the ball home.

The hosts came close again with a free kick from Matt Phillips before United slowly settled into the game. Costa came close with two crosses which did not quite reach their intended targets; Eddie Nketiah and Gjanni Alioski. Stuart Dallas also shot the ball over the bar twice.

It was real 'end to end' stuff with strong penalty claims from both sides. Casilla had certainly made amends for his earlier gaffe and was dealing with everything that the Baggies could throw at him.

Patrick Bamford and Barry Douglas replaced Eddie Nketiah and Gjanni Alioski after the break and it soon became apparent that Bamford's muscle and hold up play was adding a positive dimension to United's game.

Helder Costa won a corner, but it was only cleared as far as Jack Harrison who crossed the ball to Bamford who headed the ball towards goal. AJAYI (52) could only deflect the ball into his own net.

Once again, the teams were locked in a tight contest with both sides coming close but they remained tied at the final whistle and all in all, it was a fair result.

## League Position: 1st

"I *think we should have won the match but also, we could have lost the match. How we managed the game was good but there were chances in both boxes. Maybe our chances were a little more possible and after we built some situations that we couldn't finish in a chance.*

*I am very happy with the match we played, the kind of match we played. Two sides played the match without violence and kept within the rules.*

*Nobody wanted to take advantage or use the rules to get an advantage. West Brom are a team with good intentions, they play differently to us, it was a clash of two different styles. They have great strikers; we managed the match but we could not avoid them creating clear chances.*"

-Marcelo Bielsa

This game also turned out to be Eddie Nketiah's last showing for the Whites as Arsenal had recalled the young striker. The Londoners were unhappy with the amount of game time Nketiah was receiving.

This would always be a risk with loan players as their agenda, their agent's agenda and their parent club's agenda were unlikely to always coincide with the club who had taken out the loan.

Jack Clarke had been recalled by Spurs for the same reason, but he had enjoyed little impact in the current season and the reported fee of £9million was looking very good value for a young player with a lot to prove.

As so often happens, the next opponents were Eddie Nketiah's parent club, Arsenal. The Gunners had recently sacked Emery Unai and had appointed ex-player, Mikel Arteta, as their new manager.

After years of going for experienced managers, the large Premier League clubs were reverting to the old practice of appointing a former player. The most recent examples were Frank Lampard at Chelsea and Ole Gunnar Solskjaer at Manchester United.

Despite the fixture falling on many people's first day back at work after Christmas and the fact that it was televised, United brought a massive number of supporters to North London.

The official ticket allocation was 8,000 but United brought many more fans who settled into various parts of the Emirates Stadium and created a 'wall of noise' which must have been something very unusual to the locals.

**Arsenal 1-0 Leeds United**
6th January, 2020

*Arsenal*
Martinez, Papastathopoulos, Holding, Luiz,
Kolasinac, Guendouzi, Xhaka, Pepe (Saka 90), Ozil
(Willock 77), Nelson (Martinelli 67), Lacazette.

*Leeds United*
Meslier, Ayling (Stevens 78), White, Berardi,
Douglas, Phillips, Gotts (Dallas 60), Harrison,
Klich, Alioski (Costa 61), Bamford.

Attendance: 58,403     Referee: Anthony Taylor

Both sides had put out relatively strong sides for
this third round FA Cup encounter. Nevertheless,
Bielsa found room to hand debuts to Ilan Meslier
and Robbie Gotts and both players gave a very good
account of themselves.

Far from being intimidated by their opponents or
the fine stadium, United started the game in a very
confident fashion. So much so that an uninformed
observer would have thought that the Whites were
the Premier League side.

The dazzling moves had the Gunners on the back
foot and if they had underestimated the
Championship side before the game, they were
learning a bitter lesson.

United's counter-attacking was particularly impressive, with Bamford coming close a couple of times, grazing the crossbar on one occasion. Harrison and Alioski were both putting in typically lively performances.

At the other end, Meslier was doing everything that was expected of him and his immaculate distribution was responsible for starting several dangerous moves.

Unfortunately, the old problem of profligacy and missed chances had come back to haunt United and despite their domination, the teams went into the break with the scores level at 0-0.

Whatever Arteta said to his charges at half time, it seemed to have a dramatic effect on his team. In the second half, Arsenal brought the game to United and the Whites began to feel some pressure themselves. Lacazette came close with a free kick that clipped the crossbar, but Meslier was dealing with everything that the Gunners threw at him.

On the hour mark, Pepe put a teasing cross into the box and Berardi was only able to deflect the ball into the path of NELSON (60), who shot home. This prompted the relieved cheers of the home crowd, who had finally found their voice.

This seemed to knock the stuffing out of United at least from an attacking point of view.

Both sides played the last half hour out with a series of niggling fouls which spoiled an otherwise fine spectacle. After the final whistle, United's players received a deserved ovation from the away end.

*"In the first half, Leeds beat clearly the opponent because we cannot analyse both halves individually. One team is what it does in all the match. For me it would be easy to point at the first half as great and all we wished for before the match.*

*Obviously, we had ten chances and we didn't score. After, in the second half, we allowed the opponent to react. In one match where we have shown we were able to beat the opponent. But we must analyse the second half to grow.*

*Teams have a process, a development. In some moments, the idealists try to focus on the good things but in this moment of our team, even more because we must play important things. We must concentrate to have a regular performance.*

*I cannot answer if we are ready for the Premier League. If we lost 4-0 to Manchester United, I could not take the conclusion either."*

-Marcelo Bielsa

For several months, street art by Burley Banksy (Andy McVeigh) made appearances all over the city. I spotted this particular tribute to Bielsa at the top of Wesley Street in Beeston, as I was making my way to the Sheffield Wednesday match.

**Leeds United 0-2 Sheffield Wednesday**
11th January, 2020

*Leeds United*
Casilla, Ayling, White, Cooper, Douglas (Alioski 56), Phillips, Costa (Stevens 65), Dallas, Klich (Hernandez 66), Harrison, Bamford.

*Sheffield Wednesday*
Dawson, Urhoghide (Hutchinson 85), Iorfa, Borner, Fox, Lee, Murphy, Luongo, (Pelupessy 77) Bannan, Reach, Winnall (Nuhiu 69).

Attendance: 36,422    Referee: Oliver Langford

After their praiseworthy trip to the capital, United came back to the stark reality of the Championship, when they lost by more than a one goal margin for the first time this season.

The old ghosts of wastefulness and missed chances returned to haunt the Whites as they laboured away without reward.

By half time, the Whites could have been at least three goals up as Patrick Bamford, Jack Harrison and Helder Costa threw away glorious chances. The more the game went on, the more it looked like it was going to end as a sterile 0-0 draw.

In the second half, despite changes in personnel with the introduction of Hernandez, Stevens and Alioski, United still failed to open their account.

Worse was to come, when MURPHY (87) beat Casilla, squeezing the ball between the Spaniard and his near post. Insult to injury was then added when the giant NUHIU (90+4) scored Wednesday's second to gift the Owls an unlikely away win.

Former United boss Garry Monk had once again turned the tables on his former club and had left the Faithful wondering what might have been.

**League Position: 2nd**

*"It's true that it's a situation that we have seen before. We didn't risk losing the ball in our half during the first 85 minutes. We lost two goals in the final five minutes. This has happened a lot.*

*We know we must protect ourselves from these situations. Again, this is one mistake which we thought that we had learned to avoid."*

-Marcelo Bielsa

The next trip was to Queens Park Rangers, who were having a rather strange season.

Although they were occupying their familiar position in mid table, they were scoring a huge amount of goals.

The problem was, they were conceding goals in almost equal quantities. Their overall form was equally unpredictable. Prior to this game, they had beaten Cardiff City 6-1 and Swansea City 5-1, before losing 3-1 to neighbours Brentford.

Further piquancy was added by the fact that former United youngster Jack Clarke had joined the Hoops on loan from Spurs and was named as a substitute.

**Queens Park Rangers 1-0 Leeds United**
18th January, 2020

*Queens Park Rangers*
Kelly, Kane, Hall, Masterson, Wallace, Cameron, Amos (Scowen 74), Osayi-Samuel, Chair (Clarke 74), Eze, Wells (Pugh 83).

*Leeds United*
Casilla, Ayling, White, Cooper, Dallas (Alioski 45), Phillips, Costa, Hernandez, Klich (Stevens 87), Harrison, Bamford.

Attendance: 16,049    Referee: Peter Bankes

A toxic combination of bad luck, terrible refereeing and wastefulness once again prevented United from taking any points away from London.

In the Premier League, VAR is rightly criticised for the inconsistency of the decisions that are made. If the experiences of this game were anything to go by, United would welcome the use of the technology with open arms.

Pablo Hernandez mishit a pass to Helder Costa who managed to stretch for it but was unceremoniously upended by Lee Wallace in the penalty area. The referee, Peter Bankes, completely ignored this and waved play on.

On the halfway line, Osayi-Samuel broke away from Liam Cooper and was finally stopped at the edge of the Leeds penalty area by Pablo Hernandez who had to concede a free kick.

Eze took the free kick and the ball was deflected to WELLS (20), who brought the ball under control using both of his arms. The former Huddersfield Town man was left with a simple shot to put the Hoops ahead.

Peter Bankes chose to ignore all of United's protestations, which also fell on silent ears of the referee's colleagues. It seems that nowadays most linesmen seek a quiet life and rarely add anything other than confirming the original decision.

In the second half, United ramped up the pressure and were finally rewarded with a penalty. Bamford skipped around Kelly, who was adjudged to have made contact in bringing the striker down.

Unfortunately, it was the languid version of Patrick Bamford who stroked a weak shot into the corner, which didn't require a massive effort to save.

With the departure of Eddie Nketiah, it was not difficult for the cynics amongst us to deduce that the lack of competition in the striker department may have led to the ex-Middlesbrough man's apparent complacency. Hernandez clipped the post with a free kick, but it was clear that United were going to leave Shepherds Bush without any points.

In the dying minutes, the frustrations boiled over and Kalvin Phillips was rightly sent off for a reckless tackle on Geoff Cameron.

This result meant that United were still without a win in 2020, with constant doom and gloom lurking on social media. The success of the remaining days in the transfer window was now looking crucial if the Whites were to stop the rot.

**League Position: 2nd**

*"What supporters see is the most important. I never try to change their mind. The match and the team is our way of answering the supporters. Of course, we are in our worst moment in the Championship. We don't have to ask for anything from the supporters because we are obliged to offer them things and try to express ourselves through the play."*

-Marcelo Bielsa

# Chapter Nine
## More Mishaps

Next up was Millwall and despite the negative start to the new year, United had concluded the transfer window in a timely and successful manner.

*Incoming Players*
Elia Caprile - Chievo (Undisclosed)
Ian Poveda - Manchester City (Undisclosed)
Jean-Kevin Augustin - Red Bull Leipzig (Loan)

*Outgoing Players*
Lewie Coyle - Fleetwood Town (Undisclosed)
Conor Shaughnessy - Burton Albion (Loan)
Eunan O'Kane - Luton Town (Undisclosed)

The signing which caused the most excitement was undoubtedly Jean-Kevin Augustin from Red Bull Leipzig. The large, mobile striker had shown great promise earlier in his career with PSG and Monaco.

His spell at Leipzig was less than impressive, but it was felt that he was young enough at the age of twenty-two to get his career back on track. He was also deemed to be an ideal player to fit into United's system and came with an expensive obligation to buy, provided that the Whites were promoted at the end of the season.

**Leeds United 3-2 Millwall**
28th January, 2020

*Leeds United*
Casilla, Ayling, White, Cooper, Alioski, Klich,
Costa, Dallas, Hernandez (Shackleton 90),
Harrison, Bamford.

*Millwall*
Bialkowski, Hutchinson, Pearce (Ferguson 72),
Cooper, Romeo, Molumby, Woods, M Wallace, J
Wallace, Bradshaw (Smith 83), Bodvarsson
(Mahoney 72).

Attendance: 34,006    Referee: Darren England

Prior to the match, United had enjoyed a ten day
break whereas their opponents had been involved in
an FA Cup action at the weekend. Despite this, it
was the Whites who looked ponderous as they
failed to get off to their usual lively start.

HUTCHINSON (4) opened the scoring for the
visitors, after Millwall had forced a corner and it
was all too easy for him to head home at the far
post. This was not the start that United were hoping
for and of course, the Millwall players baited the
Elland Road crowd.

Alioski and Klich led the fightback but it was
Bamford who missed the best chance, shooting
straight at the grateful Bialkowski.

Dallas had a fine effort turned around the post by the Millwall keeper, but the referee judged that it was a goal kick. Worse was to follow though.

Ryan Woods had clearly run the ball out in front of the West Stand, but play was waved on. From the resultant cross, Cooper and Alioski were adjudged to have sandwiched Bialkowski and a penalty was awarded. JED WALLACE (23) dispatched the ball past Casilla to undeservedly double Millwall's lead.

Dallas came close for United with a header, but the teams went into the break with no change in the score line. Victor Orta and James Mooney had some harsh words with referee Darren England in the tunnel, for which they later received fines. In fact, they were merely putting into words the feelings of every Whites fan.

Just three minutes into the second half, United were awarded a corner. Hernandez swung the ball into Ayling, who then flicked it on to Harrison. Bialkowski could only parry the shot from the Manchester City loanee to BAMFORD (48), who gratefully prodded the ball home.

The goal provided the impetus that the Whites were looking for. This prompted wave after wave of attacks with Alioski, Harrison and Bamford all coming close shortly afterwards. Suddenly, the ball was bobbing about in the Millwall penalty area. When it came free to HERNANDEZ (62), he lashed a shot into the net from eighteen yards.

United then went for Millwall's throats and BAMFORD (66) stooped to head home his second and send the Elland Road crowd into raptures.

The Whites kept up the pressure and Costa was extremely unlucky to see his shot hit the bar. Klich also missed a golden opportunity after finding himself clear with only Bialkowski to beat.

There were no additional goals and the Elland Road faithful made their way home after witnessing an exciting match. The Whites not only overcame their opponents, but also the shocking standard of refereeing which could have cost them dearly.

**League Position: 1st**

*"It's not what I said which provoked the change after half time. Maybe the match looked like it was strange but it was a copy of all our matches.*

*It took a lot of chances to score three goals and the opponent's goals were like what we normally receive. At the end of the match it was uncomfortable and not calm but, in both halves, we had a lot of chances. We played very well in attack. It was like most of our matches."*

-Marcelo Bielsa

**Leeds United 0-1 Wigan Athletic**
1st February, 2020

*Leeds United*
Casilla, Ayling, White, Cooper, Alioski, Klich, Costa, Dallas, Hernandez, Harrison, Bamford (Roberts 64).

*Wigan Athletic*
Marshall, Byrne, Kipre, Dunkley, Naismith, Pearce (Jacobs 84), Evans, Morsy, Williams, Moore, Massey (Lowe 69).

Attendance: 35,162    Referee: Tony Harrington

The corresponding match last season had produced a seminal moment for United, as the defeat caused the Whites to slip to third place, a position from which they never recovered.

In the last twelve months, Wigan Athletic had only managed to win one other game away from home. This was at Birmingham City. This year, United's suffering was to continue despite the positive performance against Millwall.

Wigan looked every bit a relegation candidate and were one of the poorest sides to visit Elland Road this season. Nevertheless, they were probably encouraged by the awful conditions, as near gale-force winds swirled around the stadium.

As usual, United dominated possession but unfortunately had nothing to show from it. After weaving his way into the penalty box, Jack Harrison was extremely unlucky to see his shot rebound off the post with Marshall well beaten. Later, the winger failed to sort his legs out after receiving a clever pass from Patrick Bamford.

Bamford himself also missed a couple of good chances and by half time, serious doubts were starting to creep in and the anxiety of the crowd was palpable. Worse was to come, as a Wigan corner was caught up in the wind and found its way into the United net via HERNANDEZ (59).

Helder Costa had several forays down the right side, rounding Wigan players as if they were not there, but his final balls were poor and the Latics subsequently found it easy to clear the danger.

It became clear that United were not going to score and as they threw caution to the wind, things were almost made worse but for timely interventions by Ben White and Stuart Dallas.

**League Position: 2nd**

*"There is nothing that makes me more frustrated than not winning a match like this one. It was difficult to think how Wigan could score.*

*If I was a Leeds supporter, I would ask the manager to explain to me why what is happening is the same when we fail to get a goal and the same thing happens every match.*

*That is my big responsibility, because after eighteen matches, we have the same problem. It should have been impossible to lose this match."*

-Marcelo Bielsa

The next match was away to Nottingham Forest, who despite losing their previous game against Birmingham City, had made steady progress and were now only four points behind the Whites.

In the press conference which preceded this game, Marcelo Bielsa took nearly an hour to answer five questions. He later defended this on the grounds that he wanted the public to be clear about how and why he came to certain decisions.

One of the implied criticisms was that he hadn't played either of the two forwards who were signed during the January transfer window. Bielsa was unrepentant and reiterated how his conditioning process worked. Nevertheless, Jean-Kevin Augustin was named as a substitute at the City Ground.

**Nottingham Forest 2-0 Leeds United**
8th February, 2020

*Nottingham Forest*
Samba, Cash, Figueiredo, Worrall, Ribeiro, Sow,
Watson, Ameobi (Diakhaby 67), Lolley, Silva
(Yates 80), Grabban (Walker 90).

*Leeds United*
Casilla, Dallas, Ayling, Cooper, Alioski (Shackleton
70), White, Costa, Hernandez (Roberts 59), Klich,
Harrison, Bamford (Augustin 71).

Attendance: 29,455    Referee: Oliver Langford

Another tough game and another defeat. Ben White
looked like a fish out of water in the midfield
holding role and the return of Kalvin Phillips was
eagerly anticipated.

United dominated possession but rarely progressed
as far as the Nottingham Forest penalty area, as
attack after attack was broken up.

Ayling allowed AMEOBI (31) to slip past him into
the penalty area and although he was left exposed,
Casilla failed to narrow the angle and let another
shot in at his near post. The Spaniard later made a
good catch, only to throw the ball straight to Ben
Watson. Luckily, the Forest skipper was well off
target and United were able to breathe again.

In the second half, Roberts, Shackleton and Augustin were introduced to no discernible effect. Casilla denied Lewis Grabban as the Forest striker chose to aim the ball at the United keeper's legs, rather than hitting the ball into the gaping empty net to his right.

The Whites had only one credible chance and this came from a corner as Liam Cooper sent a bullet header towards goal. Despite his inactivity earlier, the Forest keeper Samba fisted the ball into the air before having a second crack at thumping it away.

As the minutes ticked away and United chased an equaliser, they were beaten at their own game by a Forest breakaway. Harrison failed to deal with a through ball, leaving Joe Lolley to unselfishly square it to WALKER (90+4) who gratefully tapped the ball into an empty net.

**League Position: 2nd**

"*The team made a big effort. How the team ran today and all the effort the players put in really touched me tonight. We had better players than the opponent but what we did was not enough to avoid another defeat.*

*Trying to give an explanation now is not useful. The resources the team has are enough. We cannot demand more effort from the players.*

*The responsibility is mine because clearly if you have good players and those players give all on the pitch, then the conclusions are clear. I have to understand that it is me who has to find the solutions."*

-Marcelo Bielsa

Unsurprisingly, the terminal moaners of social media were all out in force after the match. It would be easy for an outside observer to deduce that United were doomed to be relegated, rather than suffering a drop in form whilst holding second place. All the obvious questions were being asked:

"What is the point of signing Poveda and Augustin without starting them?"

"How does Bamford keep his place?"

"Surely Meslier should now start after Casilla's recent performances?"

So-called responsible journalists were also putting these questions and suggestions to Bielsa, as if they were brilliant ideas which would bring the answer to all United's problems.

Bielsa answered the questions politely, although his frustration was thinly concealed and it was obvious that he was hiding his true feelings.

To add to all of these facts, the next match was away to Brentford in the capital. Given United's recent performances against London clubs, very few people gave the Whites much hope of heading back to Yorkshire with one point, let alone three.

**Brentford 1-1 Leeds United**
11th February, 2020

*Brentford*
Raya, Dalsgaard, Jeanvier, Pinnock, Henry, Jensen (Fosu-Henry 89), Norgaard, Dasilva (Marcondes 63), Mbeumo (Baptiste 89), Watkins, Benrahma.

*Leeds United*
Casilla, Ayling, White, Cooper, Dallas, Phillips, Costa, Hernandez, Klich, Harrison, Bamford (Augustin 76).

Attendance: 12,294    Referee: Robert Jones

Brentford Manager Thomas Frank had said before the match that this fixture could not have come at a worse time for the Whites and that they must be feeling some fear, given their recent form and performances in the capital city.

A big positive for United was the return of Kalvin Phillips, who had been absent for the last three games owing to the red card which he received in the dying stages of the Queens Park Rangers match.

The Whites made a lively start and were soon on the front foot, silencing the home fans with some great attacking football. Harrison and Ayling both should have tested the Brentford goalkeeper, but their respective efforts caused him no problems at all.

As United were beginning to tighten their grip, disaster occurred. Liam Cooper sent a routine back pass to Casilla. The Spaniard had been having a torrid time of it in recent weeks but the one aspect of his game where he could usually be relied upon was his sure-footedness.

Not on this occasion unfortunately, he completely lost his balance, allowing BENRAHMA (25) to nip in and tap the ball into an empty net. It really did seem as if the London curse had struck again and the United fans behind the goal could not believe what they had just witnessed.

However, Bielsa's men made a positive response and Pablo Hernandez came close with a rising shot. Both Hernandez and Bamford spurned later chances that came along, but the Whites kept pressing.

Two corners taken by Jack Harrison followed in quick succession; The first almost found Phillips at the far post. The second was dropped by the goalkeeper, Raya, allowing COOPER (38) to smash home his first goal of the season.

Costa came close before the break and in the second half, both the ex-Wolves man and Bamford spurned genuine goal opportunities. Bamford was replaced by Jean-Kevin Augustin with fifteen minutes left, but the newcomer did not have much to offer.

Hernandez came closest, but thanks to Casilla's horrendous error, United had to settle for a draw when they really deserved to win. United had dominated so much that Brentford had only two shots on target, with one of those being the gift presented to Benrahma.

**League Position: 2nd**

*"During the match, we always took risks. Our full backs attack all the time and you must think that Brentford have three very good attackers. That meant the opposite of fear to play here. This means we wanted to win and were prepared to take risks."*

-Marcelo Bielsa

Two days later, Marcelo Bielsa held his usual pre-match press conference at Thorpe Arch. The previous week he had taken 59 minutes to answer five questions. A lesser man would have lost his temper or snapped back, but Bielsa just reiterated his philosophy for the umpteenth time to the 'deaf ears' of the British press.

Bielsa opened this week's conference by defiantly stating that Kiko Casilla would be starting against Bristol City and that all his teammates supported their beleaguered goalkeeper. This obviously anticipated some of the main questions.

Present at this conference was Mark Irwin of the Sun Newspaper, who believes that he knows better that Bielsa's admirers Pep Guardiola and Mauricio Pochettino. Irwin went on to describe Bielsa as a 'Pound Shop Unai Emery'.

Irwin pointed out that if United lost the game against Bristol City, the Whites could slip out of the automatic promotion places. He also bemoaned the fact that Bielsa did not speak good English and questioned how he could possibly motivate the players. The journalist also said that thirty minutes at the press conference was the longest thirty minutes of his life.

Returning to Unai Emery, Irwin mocked his accent and use of the phrase 'good ebening'. His xenophobic comments bordered on racism and just like Thomas Frank, provided United with extra motivation for their forthcoming match.

When I was a boy, old newspapers were cut into six-inch squares and hung from a nail in the outside toilet. It is rather a shame that Mark Irwin's article could not suffer the same fate.

# Chapter Ten
## Winning Wave

**Leeds United 1-0 Bristol City**
15th February, 2020

*Leeds United*
Casilla, Ayling, White, Cooper, Dallas, Phillips, Costa, Hernandez (Shackleton 90), Klich, Harrison, Bamford (Augustin 75).

*Bristol City*
Bentley, Kalas, Williams, Baker, Dasilva, Eliasson (Palmer 74), Massengo, Henriksen, Paterson (Diedhiou 60), Weimann (O'Dowda 34), Wells.

Attendance: 35,819    Referee: Tim Robinson

United may have only won by a single goal, but this was as a complete demolition from start to finish. The Whites dominated possession and led every other meaningful statistic by a large margin.

Even before AYLING (16) stabbed the ball into the net after a game of pinball in the Robins' penalty area, United had made their intentions clear and there was only one team in it.

Fine performances were recorded by Ayling himself as well as Phillips, Dallas, Harrison, Klich and Costa. Although the conditions were awful, United adapted better than the visitors.

Passes went astray, but the central midfield pairing Klich and Phillips mopped up the stray balls and regained possession countless times. The Whites kept up the pressure in the second half with Harrison hitting the crossbar and Costa forcing a great save from Bentley, after the Wolves loanee had skipped around him.

Like they did through much of the autumn, United produced a result without taking advantage of all the chances which were on offer.

**League Position: 2nd**

*"We attacked well but we missed a lot of chances. We defended well, they created few chances. We ran a lot, we fought for every ball. The performance in general and collectively was very positive.*

*The team controlled the match, defended very well, attacked very well. We scored just one goal but you saw all the chances the team had. We ran a lot. We recovered a lot of 50-50 balls. We have experienced every type of situation in the Championship and I feel that we have more resources to manage the different types of matches that we face."*

-Marcelo Bielsa

Next to come was the rare treat of another home Saturday game at three o'clock, with Reading being this week's visitors. The arrival of Mark Bowen had steadied their ship and they were no longer viewed as relegation candidates.

**Leeds United 1-0 Reading**
22nd February, 2020

*Leeds United*
Casilla, Ayling, White, Cooper, Dallas, Phillips (Alioski 37), Costa, Klich, Hernandez (Shackleton 85), Harrison, Bamford.

*Reading*
Cabral, Yiadom, Morrison, Moore, Richards, Pele, Rinomhota, Meite, Swift (Adam 76), Olise, Puscas.

Attendance: 35,483    Referee: Jarred Gillett

In some ways, this result was even more satisfying than the Bristol City game, as United created many fewer chances but managed to convert the vital one.

The first half followed a familiar pattern with United dominating without a goal to show for their efforts. Helder Costa came closest with a fine effort, which just passed the wrong side of the far post.

On thirty-seven minutes, the fans' anxiety levels were increased after the usually 'bulletproof' Kalvin Phillips took a heavy knock and had to leave the pitch.

This produced a shuffle which saw Dallas move to right back, Alioski drop into left back, Ayling to centre back and Ben White taking over the holding midfield role.

To the enormous credit of all concerned, not least the coaching staff, this change passed with seamless efficiency. White looked more comfortable in his new role, with honours remaining even at the break.

Hernandez had not been in the best of form, but he enjoyed a reasonable first half, managing to keep Roberts warming the bench. However, the second half saw the Spaniard back to his scintillating best.

It was just before the hour mark when Helder Costa provided the assist with a neat little flick. After smashing the ball against a Reading defender, HERNANDEZ (57) retrieved the ball, waltzed around another defender and struck the ball into the top corner.

The team's delight at this was only matched by the joy of the Elland Road crowd as once again, the little magician had found a key to unlock the most stubborn of defences.

After this, Hernandez turned on a masterclass in control and passing which showed that even a player of his experience can benefit from a confidence booster. In fact, he was enjoying himself so much that he wasn't best pleased to be replaced by Shackleton with only five minutes left.

Kiko Casilla celebrated back-to-back clean sheets, which was nearly jeopardised by a late effort from Liam Moore. Bielsa took the time to go on the pitch and congratulate the Spaniard, who was clearly fighting his way back to the form he had shown earlier in the season.

*"This match was like the matches that we are used to playing. Generally, we create double or triple the chances of the opponent. Today this was the situation. They have some attackers that are not easy to control.*

*There was a situation in the last minute for them that we should have resolved when their number six became a striker. That created confusion that we could have solved from the bench. It was this player who had a clear chance in the last minute."*

-Marcelo Bielsa

February's final outing was at the Riverside Stadium in Middlesbrough, a venue which had never been a happy hunting ground for United. The previous season, the Whites had scraped a draw with their latest equaliser ever when PHILLIPS (90+11) had sent a bullet header into the back of the net from a goalmouth scramble.

The lengthy stoppage time came as a result of Jack Clarke's health scare earlier in the game and unfortunately, the youngster's best form seems to have deserted him since.

Having demolished Middlesbrough at Elland Road, hopes were high that United could register another win although nobody was expecting such a generous margin.

**Middlesbrough 0-1 Leeds United**
27th February, 2020

*Middlesbrough*
Pears, Howson, Shotton, Moukoudi, Friend (Johnson 63), Clayton, Saville (Nmecha 67), Tavernier, Wing, Coulson, Fletcher (Assombalonga 72).

*Leeds United*
Casilla, Ayling, Berardi, Cooper, Dallas, White, Costa, Klich, Hernandez (Shackleton 73), Harrison, Bamford.

Attendance: 24,647    Referee: Gavin Ward

This match had an 'old boys' feel about it with former Elland Road favourites Jonathan Woodgate, Robbie Keane, Jonny Howson and Adam Clayton all involved for Middlesbrough.

Kalvin Phillips was absent as he had failed to recover from the heavy knock which he had picked up against Reading. This meant that the ever-reliable Gaetano Berardi stepped in to allow Ben White to move forward into central midfield.

Early on, Bamford sent a weak header straight into the welcoming arms of Aynsley Pears. Not long afterwards, Dallas also tested the Boro goalkeeper with a good shot after linking up with Hernandez.

United consistently kept up the pressure on their hosts and in the dying minutes of the first half, they were rewarded. Klich latched on to a ball and fed Bamford, who in turn let Hernandez through. The little Spanish wizard smashed the ball towards goal, only to see it bounce back of the post.

After a half-hearted clearance from Ryan Shotton, KLICH (45+1) played a quick exchange with Hernandez before scoring a fine goal off the inside of the post.

Shortly after the interval, Casilla made a flying save from George Saville, whose thirty yard shot was bang on target. Hernandez then tested Pears and the Boro keeper did not have to wait long to be called upon again, as the game swung from end to end.

Leeds-born Marcus Tavernier came closest for the home side with a shot which rattled the crossbar, while Bamford had a ball tipped off his feet by a Boro defender just two yards out from the goal. Nevertheless, United weathered the storm and produced another fine 1-0 win.

**League Position: 2nd**

*"The team fought a lot and were very aggressive. We attacked better in the second half. Today the team protected the result. We played well in different moments of the match. The team did not lose their calm and they fought. In general, we managed the situations well.*

*Maybe in some moments in the second half, Middlesbrough created some problems but in general, we had three more chances than them. There was a lot of fight in the match. We resolved well, the absence of Kalvin Phillips. We were compact and tough to play against. Scoring is the most difficult thing in football and more efficient teams do better."*

-Marcelo Bielsa

Back in September, you'll remember that United travelled to Charlton in the capital. After the game, Macauley Bonne, made a remark to the press that there had been an incident during the game which he could not speak about. All was revealed at a later date, though.

Snippets of information filtered out from the media and on November 4th, Kiko Casilla was formally charged with making a racially abusive remark to Bonne's colleague, Jonathan Leko. As is so often the case, social media was filled with all sorts of versions about what is supposed to have happened.

Of course, the vast majority of United fans found it hard to believe that their goalkeeper was capable of such an offence. It has to be said that most simply did not want to believe such a thing.

From the beginning, Casilla steadfastly denied the charges and requested a personal hearing. As a result of this, the case was not resolved until February 28th, just a day before the Whites travelled to Hull City.

The Football Association had concluded that Casilla was guilty and issued an eight match ban, with a fine of £60,000. Crucially, at this point they did not disclose their written reasons or any other information relating to the case.

As a result of this, the United fans still believed that their player must be innocent and demonstrated their solidarity with him before the Hull City game. Despite this, it was the talented youngster Illan Meslier who took Casilla's place between the sticks.

The following week, the Football Association published the reasoning behind their decision and it was difficult to see how they could have come to a different conclusion. Macauley Bonne backed Lecko and gave evidence that he clearly heard the offending remark.

Casilla's defence was inconsistent and whilst many players, including former team mate Eddie Nketiah, gave the Spaniard glowing character references, nobody could recall hearing the remark itself. The truth will never be known, but it's clear that the goalkeeper's legal advice was poor and the defence was unconvincing.

Marcelo Bielsa gave a typically wise and measured response after the findings had been published:

*"The authorities have expressed themselves. Kiko has also and so has the club. I think that any contribution that I can make is not significant. I think that we must accept the rules of the competition and accept those decisions. All of us are against every kind of discrimination and racism, this is very clear.*

*The effect this sanction has had on Kiko's spirit is clear, it is not just something professional if something has impact on his behaviour and personal matters. Kiko is a great human being and of course a situation like this affects him.*

*But I think he is strong and all of us will support him, fundamentally with the love that he deserves because I want this love between us."*

**Hull City 0-4 Leeds United**
29th February, 2020

*Hull City*
Long, McKenzie, Pennington, McLoughlin, Elder,
Stewart, Da Silva Lopes (Batty 63), Wilks,
Samuelsen (Maddison 76), Honeyman, Magennis
(Balogh 63).

*Leeds United*
Meslier, Ayling, White, Cooper, Dallas, Phillips,
Costa, Hernandez (Shackleton 88), Klich, Harrison
(Alioski 88), Bamford (Roberts 67).

Attendance: 16,178    Referee: Keith Stroud

Illan Meslier made his Championship debut in place
of Kiko Casilla and Kalvin Phillips returned to a
strong United side. By contrast, Hull City had nine
players out through injury and made four changes
from their previous game.

The pattern of the match was soon established when
AYLING (5) let fly with a twenty-five yard effort
which was deflected into the net. Shortly
afterwards, Pablo Hernandez rattled the crossbar
with a fine shot, drifting into the box after picking
up a pass from Jack Harrison.

The teams went into the break with no additional
scores, but it felt as though the Tigers would not be
able to hold the tide back for much longer.

It was the mercurial HERNANDEZ (47) who slotted home early in the second half, after receiving a nice through ball from Helder Costa.

Costa and Klich came close shortly afterwards, with both players having been set up by Jack Harrison. The Manchester City loanee was then extremely unlucky, as he had an effort strike the post himself.

United continued to besiege the Hull City defence and with just over twenty minutes left, Tyler Roberts replaced Patrick Bamford.

The Whites had scored a number of goals from breakaways earlier in the season, but the next one was arguably the best. It was both a thing of beauty and a triumph of hard work and determination.

Phillips regained possession in the United penalty area, before releasing the ball to Stuart Dallas. Both Dallas and Jack Harrison found themselves hemmed in right on the touchline, but somehow they scraped their way clear with quick exchanges. Most players in this situation would be content on playing the ball against an opponent and be glad of a throw in.

Harrison then shot off down the wing before finding Klich and the Pole slid a beautiful pass into the box, where ROBERTS (81) was there to smash it in. Three minutes later, Klich once again sent in a killer cross and ROBERTS (84) netted with a beautifully placed header. This was a comprehensive victory which showed United at their scintillating best.

**League Position: 2nd**

*"I want to tell you that we value the result of today but we know that we played against a team that sold its best two players and in addition they had five or six players injured. I thought that at my age, I could be more relaxed regarding the consequence of my job but the opposite has happened. I am very worried about what is going to happen.*

*I do not need to worry about what is going to happen, I have to analyse what is going to happen. I always analyse, but I feel harm when something is not going well, even if the analysis is positive."*

-Marcelo Bielsa

Before the next match, Huddersfield Town's most recent visit came in September 2016. On that occasion, the Terriers ran out 1-0 winners in what proved to be a pivotal result in their promotion season. It would appear that this particular game's importance had not faded in three-and-a-half years.

Just a day before the next instalment, the Terriers posted pictures on social media of their players celebrating Aaron Mooy's winner with the caption: "Last time at Elland Road…"

Unsurprisingly, this tweet backfired and received numerous replies from United fans following the final whistle of 'this time at Elland Road'.

**Leeds United 2-0 Huddersfield Town**
7th March, 2020

*Leeds United*
Meslier, Ayling, Berardi, Cooper, Dallas, White,
Costa, Hernandez, Klich (Shackleton 83), Harrison
(Alioski 90+3), Bamford (Roberts 79).

*Huddersfield Town*
Lossl, Simpson, Stearman, Schindler, Toffolo,
Chalobah, O'Brien, Willock (Pritchard 64), Rowe
(Bacuna 72), Grant, Campbell (Mounie 61).

Attendance: 36,514    Referee: Oliver Langford

United got off to the perfect start when Jack
Harrison floated the ball across the penalty area and
AYLING (3) launched himself at the ball, in what
can only be described as a flying volley.

The defender's effort went in off the crossbar and
sent the home crowd into ecstasies. Incredibly, this
took the ex-Bristol City man to three goals out of
his last five games.

Meslier was rarely tested in the first half, although
he did catch one ball between his legs, which he
cheekily produced from behind his back. This
youngster is certainly a cool customer! In the
second half, Pablo Hernandez produced an inviting
free kick, which Lossl somehow managed to parry
away to BAMFORD (52), who gratefully tapped it
into the net.

Like the previous match, Harrison hit the woodwork when he unleashed a rasping shot. The rebound fell to Hernandez, who saw his effort blocked.

Once again, United registered a convincing win and were seven points clear of third place Fulham, with just nine games remaining.

**League Position: 1st**

*"It was a match where we defended well, we didn't receive real chances, just the one in the first half. In attack, we could have scored maybe one more goal. Anyway the team did very well in attack as well.*

*I don't realise difference in performance but I can see a difference in efficiency."*

-Marcelo Bielsa

# Chapter Eleven
## Distant Days

Even the more pessimistic fans accepted that the
Hull City and Huddersfield Town matches saw
United at the top of their game. The unbeaten run
appeared to be gaining a head of steam and others
were expressing the view that promotion to the top
tier was almost inevitable.

Then disaster struck and the world was about to
change forever. The storm clouds that had been
gathering in faraway places suddenly came much
nearer to home. Within a week of the Huddersfield
triumph, all domestic football was suspended and
the season was brought to a sudden halt.

Social media was filled with comments from
stunned fans bemoaning that yet again, having come
within sight of the winning post, United were about
to have the prize snatched from them.

Almost as soon as lockdown and the cessation of
hostilities were announced, people soon realised
that there were greater issues at stake. As the cases
of COVID-19 soared and the death rate grew daily,
families lost members, and people lost their
livelihoods.

Panic buying erupted in the supermarkets, with everything from toilet rolls to alcohol being cleared from the shelves by the mindlessly selfish members of our society. Thankfully though, these actions were counterbalanced by the many stories of self-sacrifice and heroism in the wider community.

The football world did not do itself any favours either. Leaders of clubs who were in danger of relegation called for the season to be declared null and void in a blatant and disgraceful display of self-interest. Many of those whose clubs were in a good position called for the season to be ended and the final table to be decided on a points-per-game basis.

As they were top of the table, the latter course of action would have benefited United, but to the credit of the Elland Road hierarchy they stuck to the view that the season should be completed whenever this would be possible.

During the lockdown, United lost two of their illustrious former players; Norman Hunter on 17th April and Trevor Cherry on 29th April. Their passing was made all the more sad as they could not be mourned properly by friends and fans because of the restrictions in place of funeral attendees.

Hunter played in 726 games and was an integral part of Don Revie's successful side, winning League Championships, domestic cups and European competitions.

His contributions were widely recognised as he was the first ever winner of the PFA Players' Player of the Year award in 1974.

Cherry joined in 1972 and went on to play 486 times for United. During his spell at Elland Road, he acquired a League Championship winners' medal and following Billy Bremner's departure, became captain in 1976.

On 16th May, the Bundesliga restarted behind closed doors and all eyes were on the opening game between Borussia Dortmund and Schalke, played in an echoing empty stadium. Unsurprisingly, England soon followed suit, with the Premier League and Championship resumption scheduled for the third week of June.

**Cardiff City 2-0 Leeds United**
21st June, 2020

*Cardiff City*
Smithies, Sanderson, Morrison, Nelson, Bennett, Bacuna, Vaulks (Tomlin 84), Ralls (Pack 75), Adomah (Mendez-Laing 65), Paterson (Glatzel 65), Hoilett (Smith 83).

*Leeds United*
Meslier, Ayling (Alioski 62), White, Cooper, Dallas, Phillips, Costa (Poveda 77), Roberts, Klich (Gotts 84), Harrison, Bamford.

Referee: Andy Woolmer

United started the game slowly but soon got into their rhythm. They dominated the possession without throwing any killer punches and then tragedy struck.

The usually composed Kalvin Phillips gave the ball away unnecessarily, passing the ball straight into the path of HOILETT (35). The former QPR man burst into the penalty area and gratefully buried the ball into the top corner, giving the exposed Meslier no chance of saving it.

This did not seem to put the Whites out of their stride unduly and they continued to press the Bluebirds back with wave after wave of attack.

Cardiff's Yorkshire born goalkeeper, Alex Smithies, was of course on top form as the Whites piled on the pressure.

In the second half, Tyler Roberts came very close to scoring after latching on to a deftly placed flicked header from Patrick Bamford. Unfortunately, the ever reliable Smithies was on hand to thwart the youngster and you began to wonder whether it was going to be one of those days.

These pessimistic thoughts were duly confirmed when GLATZEL (71) doubled the home side's lead. This was the result of another gift, this time from Liam Cooper.

From then on, United never looked like equalising. They were missing the creative spark of Pablo Hernandez as they toiled away with out any reward for their efforts.

**League Position: 2nd**

*"It was a good opportunity for us but we could not take advantage. It was a strange match, not normal. They shot twice and scored twice.*

*Another thing we could have resolved was the unbalanced situation in the middle of the pitch. We think that for all the possession and control that we had, we could have created clearer chances both in quality and quantity."*

-Marcelo Bielsa

The remaining eight matches were now going to follow each other at the rate of two per week as the season raced towards its conclusion.

Fulham were the first visitors to Elland Road since the resumption of hostilities and with more than 15,000 cardboard 'crowdies' seated in the stadium, the scene was set for a very important fixture. This had been talked up as a 'must win' game for United and for once it was hard to argue with this rating.

As the Whites were struggling against Cardiff on the previous Sunday, the Cottagers had already given three points away to local rivals Brentford.

Nevertheless, Fulham could move to within four points of the Whites, while a United win would broaden the gap to ten points. Brentford had managed to squeeze Fulham into fourth place, so a victory for the men from SW6 would be even more important to them.

**Leeds United 3-0 Fulham**
27th June, 2020

*Leeds United*
Meslier, Ayling, White, Cooper, Dallas, Phillips, Costa (Alioski 45), Klich (Douglas 80), Roberts, Harrison (Poveda 83), Bamford (Hernandez 45) (Shackleton 90+2).

*Fulham*
Rodak, Odoi, Hector, Ream, Bryan (Le Marchand 75), Reed, Arter (Kebano 63), Knockaert (Cavaleiro 70), Cairney (Johansen 75), Decordova-Reid (Onomah 75), Mitrovic.

Referee: Tony Harrington

United started the game unchanged and this came as no surprise despite the availability of the Spanish wizard, Pablo Hernandez.

The game was less than two minutes old when Mitrovic deliberately elbowed Ben White in the face. This could not possibly be construed as anything other than a serious foul and the Serbian was lucky that the referee was unsighted.

Thankfully, Mitrovic was later banned for three games after the footage had been reviewed by the EFL authorities.

United started with a flourish and BAMFORD (10) scored a well taken goal with his left foot. Helder Costa had provided the assist as he shrugged off defenders with a mazy run, before crossing the ball from the right.

As the game wore on, Fulham squeezed their way back into the game and finished the first half with more than 60% of the possession.

At half time, Bielsa made an inspired double substitution, bringing in Pablo Hernandez and Gjanni Alioski for Patrick Bamford and Helder Costa. The effect, as the Smirnoff advertisement used to say, was shattering! Both of United's second half goals came from counter-attacks.

Once again, great running from Jack Harrison culminated in a cross which evaded the Fulham defence, but not ALIOSKI (56) who had time to trap the ball before smashing it into the net.

Pablo Hernandez then picked out HARRISON (71) with a fine pass. The Manchester City loanee got behind the Fulham defence and jinked his way through the remaining challenges, before slotting the ball through the legs of the advancing Rodak.

This was United at their scintillating best and more than made up for the Cardiff disappointment.

**League Position: 1st**

*"In the first half, it was difficult to keep the ball after we recovered it. So I thought we must try a different option with Tyler Roberts and Pablo Hernandez to manage the attack of the team better.*

*When Pablo came on, it improved the performance of the team. He had a long period without playing so we thought the better option was that 45 minutes was enough."*

-Marcelo Bielsa

Next up was Luton Town at Elland Road. The Hatters were firmly anchored at the foot of the table but had experienced better form of late. The 'dead cat bounce' had been achieved by the appointment of their former manager Nathan Jones.

Jones had been sacked in the autumn after a miserable run as manager of Stoke City, where he had clearly been out of his depth. His slow and agonising demise was referred to in the second chapter of this book, but nobody could deny that he had been given a fair length of time to impose himself on the Stoke job.

**Leeds United 1-1 Luton Town**
30th June, 2020

*Leeds United*
Meslier, Ayling, White, Cooper (Berardi 12)
(Alioski 45), Dallas (Shackleton 90+4), Phillips,
Costa, Klich (Hernandez 61), Roberts, Harrison,
Bamford.

*Luton Town*
Sluga, Bree, Pearson, Carter-Vickers, Bradley,
Potts, Tunnicliffe, Cranie (Collins 64), Mpanzu,
Hylton (Bolton 64), McManaman (Cornick 45).

Referee: John Brooks

In the opening stages, a Luton free kick evaded
Meslier, who appeared to have been pushed from
behind. In the ensuing melee, Liam Cooper
overstretched himself in the scramble to clear the
ball. The big centre back then limped off after only
twelve minutes to be replaced by the ever-reliable
Gaetano Berardi.

The Bedfordshire side had clearly come to Elland
Road with the intention of 'parking the bus' as
attack after attack from the Whites fizzled out
around the half way line.

Costa and Roberts did have efforts on goal which
flew over the crossbar and a constant succession of
fruitless corners only added to the frustration.

After the break, Bielsa gambled on the attacking prowess of Alioski who came on for Berardi.

Luton's first real attack produced a goal. Substitute CORNICK (50) was tracked and forced wide by Ben White, but not wide enough to prevent his angled shot from flashing past Meslier and into the top corner. It's not often that the Brighton loanee is beaten in this fashion, but you did feel that he had backed off the striker for too long and should have got a tackle in.

This was a signal for United to lay siege to the Luton goal with good efforts from Roberts and Costa. Kalvin Phillips then fired a free kick from the edge of the area after Bamford had been brought down. Sluga parried it as far as Costa who hit the side netting with his second attempt.

Just after the hour mark, Pablo Hernandez was introduced and had an almost immediate effect on the game. Despite being completely surrounded, the little Spaniard picked out Gjanni Alioski who threaded the ball through to DALLAS (63). The Irishman made no mistake as Luton's defence was finally breached.

Shortly afterwards, Dallas returned the compliment with a good assist but Alioski could only find the side netting with his header.

It was another point closer to United's eventual goal as well as being a good recovery and a spirited performance against a side fighting for survival. Of course, the negative keyboard warriors could not see it that way and murmured about 'bottling it' along with other meaningless phrases.

**League Position: 1st**

*"Obviously, we lost two points. Points that were difficult to lose. We had to miss fifteen chances but football is like that. In the first half, how the players were placed wasn't convenient.*

*Second half, the couple of Alioski and Harrison made more things than Dallas and Harrison. The same thing happened on the right side with Costa and Dallas. Three defenders was enough with Ayling, Phillips and White.*

*Berardi defended very well in the first period. He was flexible, didn't make any fouls and was quick with the ball. But when I decided to take him off and put Alioski on, that allowed Dallas to attack more than Ayling on the right and Alioski more than Dallas on the left."*

-Marcelo Bielsa

**Blackburn Rovers 1-3 Leeds United**
4th July, 2020

*Blackburn Rovers*
Walton, Nyambe, Lenihan, Adarabioyo, Bennett
(Downing 22), Travis (Davenport 69), Johnson,
Rothwell (Buckley 69), Gallagher (Graham 60),
Holtby (Samuel 60), Armstrong.

*Leeds United*
Meslier, Ayling, White, Cooper, Douglas, Phillips,
Harrison, Roberts (Hernandez 61), Klich
(Shackleton 89), Alioski, Bamford.

Referee: Robert Jones

The resilient Liam Cooper had thankfully recovered
from the injury which he sustained against Luton.
Stuart Dallas and Helder Costa were not so
fortunate and were replaced by Barry Douglas and
Gjanni Alioski.

Watching this game on LUTV seemed all the more
poignant as this is one of the away matches that
always carries a big allocation of tickets. Seven or
eight thousand United fans can always be relied
upon to create the right sort of atmosphere.

The Whites started well after Klich had
dispossessed Lewis Travis about thirty yards from
the Rovers goal. The Polish midfielder then
threaded the ball into BAMFORD (7) who calmly
slotted it into the bottom corner.

United continued to press and good work from Ben White resulted in a corner. Barry Douglas had two bites of the cherry and his second effort found Tyler Roberts via Gjanni Alioski.

The youngster had his feet taken away from him as Holtby desperately tried to intervene. After a short conversation with Douglas, PHILLIPS (40) stepped up and sent a fine rising shot into the top corner. It was United's first direct goal from a free kick since Pablo Hernandez's strike against Burton Albion on Boxing Day 2017.

Shortly after the break, Rovers had a successful free kick of their own. Kalvin Phillips was adjudged to have fouled Armstrong just outside the box. United's current favourite son argued strongly that he was trying to get out of the way, but the referee would not be influenced.

ARMSTRONG (48) left Meslier stranded with a fine shot which was very similar to the one that Phillips had buried in the first half.

Thankfully, the Whites didn't have time to become fearful or anxious as KLICH (53) sent in a bouncing shot which evaded Rovers keeper Christian Walton.

To the very end, Bielsa was urging his men to continue to attack and by this time, Blackburn Rovers looked like a veteran heavyweight boxer swaying on the ropes.

**League Position: 1st**

*"Every match in this period is very important and every distraction for us is very important if we lose track. We are made to pay for every distraction so we need to keep focused on each match."*

-Marcelo Bielsa

Hot on the heels of the Blackburn game came the encounter with Stoke City. The Potters were still struggling despite the appointment of the former Northern Ireland boss, Michael O'Neill. Stoke were something of an enigma, having just trounced fellow strugglers Barnsley 4-0, despite losing 3-0 a few days earlier to Wigan Athletic.

**Leeds United 5-0 Stoke City**
9th July, 2020

*Leeds United*
Meslier, Ayling, White, Cooper (Berardi 84), Dallas (Douglas 75), Phillips, Costa, Roberts (Hernandez 45), Klich (Shackleton 78), Harrison (Alioski 78), Bamford.

*Stoke City*
Butland, Smith, Collins (Chester 45), Batth, Martins Indi, McClean, Campbell (Gregory 61), Cousins, Clucas (Thompson 82), Powell (Sorensen 75), Vokes (Diouf 62).

Referee: Darren Bond

This performance brought United back to the form that they had shown against Huddersfield and Hull before the season was brought to a halt.

Stoke City deployed five players across the back and it was clear that they would have been happy to return to the Potteries with a single point.

Within thirty seconds of the start, United had stated their own intentions when Tyler Roberts brought the best out of Potters keeper Jack Butland. The former United loanee was happy to tip the ball round the post and out of danger.

James McClean was also called upon to clear Bamford's shot off the line and as the pressure mounted, the visitors were made to look more and more desperate by the rampant but patient Whites.

As half time was looming, Smith inexplicably upended Helder Costa in the penalty area. This was unnecessary as the United man was heading out of the box and landed well outside the area.

KLICH (45) stepped up and calmly stroked the penalty into the right hand corner, sending Butland the wrong way.

The Whites began the second half in characteristic style and COSTA (47) seemed to have all the time in the world to trap the ball before toe-poking it into the net.

Pablo Hernandez sent one of his trademark passes across to Kalvin Phillips on the right before popping up on that side of the pitch himself, retrieving the ball and sending a perfect pass to COOPER (57) who slotted the ball home gleefully.

HERNANDEZ (72) then added his name to the scoresheet, stroking in a peach from all of twenty yards. As the stunned Potters floundered, Bielsa urged his charges forward, shouting "Again, again."

BAMFORD (90+3) had his selfless performance rewarded when he raced on to Luke Ayling's through ball to score one of his own. The ball bounced off both posts leaving the bemused Butland stranded.

**League Position: 1st**

*"Both halves were different. We started the match well. But the second part of the first half we lost contact with the opponent's goal and therefore scoring at the end of the first half was important.*

*The second half early goal made the match easier but in any case, it was a good result. It was not a match with five goals difference between the two teams."*

-Marcelo Bielsa

# Chapter Twelve
## Rightful Return

The next game was against Swansea City at the Liberty Stadium. The last time United had beaten the Swans on their turf was 56 years ago, when they were known as Swansea Town and played their games at the Vetch Field.

Twenty-four hours before the next instalment with the Welsh side, we received the sad news that another of Revie's famous team, Jack Charlton, had passed away. Charlton remains United's record appearance holder with 773 games, a feat which will surely never be surpassed.

Yorkshire's favourite Geordie acquired League Championship, FA Cup, League Cup and European medals in his time at Elland Road. But arguably his most notable achievement was his involvement in England's only World Cup winning side in 1966.

Charlton also had spells in charge of Middlesbrough, Sheffield Wednesday and Newcastle United. However, his managerial career will always be remembered for his work with the Republic of Ireland national side.

Before the arrival of 'Big Jack' in 1985, the Boys in Green had never qualified for a major tournament. During his reign, they reached the knockout stages of the 1990, 1994 and 2002 World Cups.

A keen fisherman as well, Charlton owned a house in Ballina, County Mayo and would often plot up on either the River Moy or Lough Conn. As a tribute, a statue of him sits at Cork Airport with his rod. He was truly admired on both sides of the Irish sea with freedom of Dublin, while being widely regarded as an honorary Loiner.

Back in 1964, travelling from Leeds to Swansea was a bit of a trek as there were no motorways. My late brother, Pat, as well as David Drake and some other pals and myself were lucky enough to make the journey.

Our Wallace Arnold coach left The Calls at midnight on Friday and didn't arrive at the Vetch Field until Saturday at two o'clock, having stopped at a couple of transport cafes on the way.

United won the game 3-0 through a Johnny Giles goal and Alan Peacock brace, which confirmed promotion to the top tier of English football. The game was also notable as a young Terry Cooper made his debut in place of the injured midfielder Albert Johanneson.

As the coach did not pick us up for the return journey until midnight, we walked the short distance to the town centre and patiently waited for the pubs to open at half past five.

David Drake spotted Jack Charlton who was holding a couple of bottles of champagne behind his back. Naturally, we followed him and Don Revie as they entered a small pub.

The rest of the team, along with chairman Harry Reynolds were inside and quite happy to buy us scruffy youths a pint of Hancock's mild each.

Revie also got all of the players to sing 'for they are jolly good fellows' in our honour. After this, we went with the team to the railway station.

For many years, I believed that we were incredibly lucky to be present in the pub where the team were drinking, but I later discovered that Revie and the boys had toured several pubs buying up the champagne to drink on the train back to Leeds.

Despite everything that happened subsequently, this remains my favourite Leeds United memory because this was the start of a magnificent dynasty. The 'laughing stock' team in a rugby league city was soon to become famous in world football.

Back to 2020 and it was not mathematically possible for the Whites to seal their fate by winning this game, as Brentford continued to snap at the heels of United and West Bromwich Albion.

Nevertheless a win would strengthen United's position and provide a fitting tribute to Jack Charlton and the others who had gone before him.

**Swansea City 0-1 Leeds United**
12th July, 2020

*Swansea City*
Woodman (Mulder 90+4), Cabango, Guehi (Celina 90+1), Naughton, Roberts, Fulton (Byers 90+1), Grimes, Bidwell (Cullen 90+1), Gallagher, Ayew, Brewster (Routledge 81).

*Leeds United*
Meslier, Ayling, White, Cooper, Dallas (Alioski 45), Phillips, Costa (Shackleton 90+3), Klich, Roberts (Hernandez 45), Harrison (Berardi 90+6), Bamford.

Referee: Keith Stroud

This was always going to be a tough encounter and as the game wore on, many fans would have reluctantly accepted a draw and the fairy tale ending to honour Big Jack did not seem likely to happen.

The match was not a pretty spectacle either and United had registered 60% possession by half time.

This was low by their standards and reduced further before the final whistle was blown. With few exceptions, the first half consisted of United pushing the Swans back but many attacks were broken up in the middle of the field.

Gjanni Alioski and Pablo Hernandez replaced Stuart Dallas and Tyler Roberts after the break and although United's movement looked sharper, there were still no tangible results for their efforts.

Illan Meslier tipped a fierce shot from Conor Gallagher over the bar and Patrick Bamford came close at the other end. Then Luke Ayling showed his stamina with a trademark run up the right wing.

He pulled the ball back to HERNANDEZ (89), who somehow found a space in the left hand corner of Woodman's goal. The bench erupted and Meslier ran the length of the pitch to congratulate the shirtless Spaniard along with his teammates.

Amidst the mayhem, Marcelo Bielsa cut a sober and expressionless figure as he watched his team edge closer to their objective.

**League Position: 1st**

*"The match was very close, very narrow with few chances. As the match progressed, our opportunities were growing.*

*In the last thirty minutes I think we deserved to impose to score and get the difference that we got at the end.*

*We are feeling more relaxed, more light because we are taking the steps that we had to. Of course, when you score at the end it's a higher feeling but the bigger emotion, we didn't get this as yet."*

-Marcelo Bielsa

Once again, United were compelled to play their fixtures after West Bromwich Albion and Brentford. The Baggies had faltered again, drawing with Fulham, whereas Brentford continued to pile the pressure on the top two after overcoming Charlton Athletic. The Whites needed to beat Barnsley to maintain their six point cushion over Brentford.

**Leeds United 1-0 Barnsley**
16th July, 2020

*Leeds United*
Meslier, Ayling, Berardi, Cooper, Dallas, Cooper, White, Harrison (Struijk 61), Costa (Alioski 49), Roberts (Hernandez 45) (Shackleton 90), Bamford.

*Barnsley*
Walton, Ludewig, Sollbauer, Andersen, Williams (Oduor 84), Mowatt, Halme (Thomas 45), Styles, Woodrow, Brown (Schmidt 78), Chaplin.

Referee: Jarred Gillett

Nobody was under the illusion that this would be anything other than a challenge despite Barnsley's lowly position in the table. United were without Kalvin Phillips, who had been informed that he would play no further part in the season, owing to the injury that he sustained at Swansea.

Unlike Luton Town a couple of weeks earlier, Barnsley had come to attack. Knowing that they had nothing to lose, the Tykes threw caution to the wind and took the game to United.

Although Barnsley took the initiative, their attacking was pretty innocuous as they set up a series of moves which faltered as they reached the final third.

Mads Andersen did come close with a glancing header from a corner but soon after, the visitors found themselves behind. Mateusz Klich sent Patrick Bamford haring towards the byline and the striker sent a killer pass into the path of the retreating SOLLBAUER (28), who could only slide the ball into his own net.

The goal did little to calm United's nerves as Bielsa continued to alter the formation in an attempt to combat Barnsley's increasingly desperate endeavours.

Pablo Hernandez replaced Tyler Roberts after the break, but even the little magician was having difficulty breaking through the Barnsley defence.

On the hour, Pascal Struijk replaced Jack Harrison and slotted in to the centre of midfield. After an initial wobble, the young Dutchman settled nicely into the game and sent Gjanni Alioski away with a fine pass. Patrick Bamford met the cross, forcing a good save from Barnsley keeper Jack Walton.

At the other end, Meslier was on hand to tip over Cauley Woodrow's shot. The youngster has a very calm demeanour and seems to be growing in confidence with every game.

Finally, it was all over. The game had been torturous to watch as it seemed a long time since United had to hang on in a game like that. Although the Swansea game had been won by a similar margin, the sense of 'manning the barricades' was not there as the Whites had kept the momentum going forward in that encounter.

The players celebrated in a way that said they knew how close this win had brought them to their objective. Not so with Bielsa; after doing the decent thing with his opposite number Gerhard Struber, he left the field in his usual expressionless manner.

**League Position: 1st**

*"It was a product of the collective effort. We had to run a lot to keep the result. I value a lot, the courage and the effort all the players gave to keep the difference in the result.*

*Until we resolve the situation mathematically it is not convenient to talk about the Premier League."*

-Marcelo Bielsa

The following day, United's neighbours Huddersfield Town were at home to West Bromwich Albion. Anything other than a win for the Baggies would mean that Elland Road would be hosting Premier League football next season.

Although the United players had kept to the line that other team's results did not concern them, they are human beings after all. According to Liam Cooper, they had organised an impromptu screening of the match at Elland Road. From subsequent clips on social media, it seemed that they had organised the opening of one of the bars as well!

Chris Willock scored an early goal for the Terriers but Dara O'Shea equalised for the Baggies just before half time.

As the game drew towards its conclusion, although you knew that a draw would be enough, there was always the possibility that West Brom would score the winner. Indeed, they had been doing so with annoying regularity throughout the season.

But as the history books will say, Arsenal loanee Emile Smith-Roe netted for Town and within ten minutes, United's promotion to the Premier League was confirmed.

I was watching the game on television myself and although I was pleased with the result, the enormity of the occasion did not sink in until the following morning when I saw the images on social media of our players celebrating this wonderful achievement.

Bielsa was at home in Wetherby, being spotted leaving his apartment not long after. He thanked well-wishers in his modest way before making the short trip to Elland Road to join the celebrations.

He was clearly emotional himself and embraced the players as they whirled around in a crazy dance of delight. Showing their qualities of recovery from emotion and a drop or two of alcohol, the players had welcomed their mentor to Thorp Arch by chanting his name.

The serious business of United's trip to Pride Park to meet their old rivals was still unfinished business. You would have to possess a vivid imagination to guess how training went on that momentous Saturday morning as well!

Over in Staffordshire, Brentford visited Stoke City, just nine days after United thrashed the Potters at Elland Road. Unsurprisingly, the Bees were widely expected to win.

Had Brentford won, United's enthronement as worthy champions would have been postponed until the Derby County match at the earliest.

Armed with the knowledge that they couldn't prevent the Whites from being promoted, Brentford would leapfrog West Bromwich Albion into second place if they avoided defeat against Stoke. The emphasis was now on the Bees and as we all know, the pressure was too great and the West London side could not withstand it.

The Potters took the lead unspectacularly in the 38th minute; which the home side hung on to and confirmed their safety from relegation. It was a great achievement for Michael O'Neill, who took over a team which had only taken eight points from their previous sixteen games under Nathan Jones.

More importantly, it handed the Championship title to United with two games remaining.

**Derby County 1-3 Leeds United**
19th July, 2020

*Derby County*
Roos, Bogle, Davies, Clarke, Forsyth (Buchanan 64), Rooney, Bird (Marriott 82), Waghorn, Sibley (Shinnie 65), Lawrence (Knight 7), Martin.

*Leeds United*
Casilla, Dallas, White, Berardi (Ayling 33), Douglas, Struijk, Poveda (Harrison 77), Hernandez, Shackleton, Alioski, Roberts (Bamford 82).

Referee: Oliver Langford

Any worries about an 'after the Lord Mayor's show' effect were soon dispelled. This was unsurprising given the vigorous celebrations that had taken place during the previous two days.

As is the custom, a Guard of Honour was formed by the home side, as United took to the field for the first time as Champions.

Despite the changes, United got off on the front foot and had the best of the early chances. Tyler Roberts tested Roos with a good shot and Ian Poveda had the ball in the net, but was ruled out for offside.

Gaetano Berardi had ended the game for Tom Lawrence robustly (but fairly), only to find that his all-action style was his own downfall as he fell awkwardly and left the field on a stretcher after only 38 minutes.

The second half produced an early goal for Derby as MARTIN (54) slotted home after Ian Poveda had failed to clear the ball. The Rams lead was short-lived though as HERNANDEZ (56) had a shot from the edge of the box blocked, but made no mistake with his second attempt.

Less than twenty minutes later, Tyler Roberts sent a through ball which Pablo Hernandez himself would have been proud of. SHACKLETON (75) raced through and calmly stroked the ball into the net for his first senior goal.

The Whites continued to apply the pressure to a jaded home side and it was therefore no surprise when Alioski's killer cross was turned into his own net by CLARKE (84).

For United, it was a further round of celebrations after victory against another rival.

**League Position: 1st (Champions)**

*"I'm very happy. People have been waiting for this promotion for a long time so it is not difficult to imagine the happiness that people are feeling now.*

*The trophy makes me happy but I have been in football for forty years so one trophy doesn't really change the percentage of trophies I have won.*

*What makes me happy is that I have won with this group of players. What got the promotion was the fantastic ability of the players."*

-Marcelo Bielsa

The season concluded against Charlton Athletic at Elland Road. The Addicks were managed by former United favourite Lee Bowyer and the Londoners had found themselves in the relegation zone.

Bowyer must have known in his heart of hearts that he was unlikely to receive any favours from his old club, as it was clear that Bielsa was in no mood to take his foot off the gas pedal.

**Leeds United 4-0 Charlton Athletic**
22nd July, 2020

*Leeds United*
Meslier, Ayling, White, Cooper, Klich (Bogusz 73), Struijk, Dallas, Harrison (Stevens 73), Hernandez (Shackleton 63), Alioski (Poveda 62), Bamford (Roberts 45).

*Charlton Athletic*
Phillips, Matthews, Lockyer, Pearce (Morgan 45), Sarr, Doughty, Cullen, McGeady (Williams 45), Field, Davison (Aneke 45), Bonne (Green 79).

Referee: Geoff Eltringham

It was clear from the starting line up that United were taking this one seriously, as the team represented their strongest available selections.

They were to be presented with the trophy after the match, but there was one final job to be done before this could take place. What followed was some beautiful football, exquisite goals and the celebration of their triumph at the end.

It didn't take long for United to grab the initiative and when the first goal came, it was a collector's piece. WHITE (13) took control of a loose ball just outside the penalty area, controlled it on his chest and sent a superb volley into the top corner.

The next goal was equally pleasing but in a different way. Pablo Hernandez, who was in fine form sent a nutmegged assist which DALLAS (28) was delighted to run for. The Irishman struck the ball into the bottom left corner with the outside of his foot.

The contest was practically over not long after the restart when ROBERTS (51) headed home a near post cross directly from a corner.

Ian Poveda was having a fine game and doing a lot to justify United's faith in him. He seems to be glued to the ball and when he sent SHACKLETON (66) away, the youngster was happy to score his second goal in two games.

As the clock ran down and with the crazy pendulum of the Championship constantly swinging, both Bowyer and his players knew that they were doomed. As the United players embraced one another at full time, the Charlton men sank to the floor in collective misery.

There were celebrations in the second city as well, with West Bromwich Albion clinching the second automatic promotion place despite being held at home by Queens Park Rangers.

The Baggies certainly made things difficult for themselves since the season's restart, but many would argue that their promotion was deserved as they've occupied a top two place since October.

Although the Hawthorns side spent most of the campaign in top spot, United won the title by ten points, confirmed in the final league table below.

| Position | Team | Played | Points |
|---|---|---|---|
| 1 (C) | Leeds United | 46 | 93 |
| 2 (P) | West Bromwich Albion | 46 | 83 |
| 3 | Brentford | 46 | 81 |
| 4 (P) | Fulham | 46 | 81 |
| 5 | Cardiff City | 46 | 73 |
| 6 | Swansea City | 46 | 70 |
| 7 | Nottingham Forest | 46 | 70 |
| 8 | Millwall | 46 | 68 |
| 9 | Preston North End | 46 | 66 |
| 10 | Derby County | 46 | 64 |
| 11 | Blackburn Rovers | 46 | 63 |
| 12 | Bristol City | 46 | 63 |
| 13 | Queens Park Rangers | 46 | 58 |
| 14 | Reading | 46 | 56 |
| 15 | Stoke City | 46 | 56 |
| 16 | Sheffield Wednesday | 46 | 56 |
| 17 | Middlesbrough | 46 | 53 |
| 18 | Huddersfield Town | 46 | 51 |
| 19 | Luton Town | 46 | 51 |
| 20 | Birmingham City | 46 | 50 |
| 21 | Barnsley | 46 | 49 |
| 22 (R) | Charlton Athletic | 46 | 48 |
| 23 (R) | Wigan Athletic | 46 | 47* |
| 24 (R) | Hull City | 46 | 45 |

*Deducted 12 Points

The results on the final day confirmed that this season's play offs would consist of two West London teams and two Welsh sides. After overcoming the outfits from South Wales over two legs, Brentford and Fulham battled for a place in the Premier League next season.

This was a clash won by the Cottagers after extra time, with Fulham left back Joe Bryan scoring twice. As a result, former Leeds United academy player, Tom Cairney, lifted the play off trophy in an eerie Wembley Stadium.

When the Championship trophy was presented to United, songs were sung, tears were shed and even the stoic Bielsa looked rapturously happy as he was persuaded by his team to lift the cup. Outside, the fireworks exploded and the locked out crowd cheered. Although they had been asked to stay away, nobody could begrudge them their celebrations.

Marcelo Bielsa did not speak to any journalists after the Charlton game, feeling that he had said everything previously while not wanting to deflect any of the praise away from his team.

# Chapter Thirteen
## Family Feeling

As a big club, United have always had celebrity fans and followers from all over the world. I also take my hat off to those who never miss a game and make great sacrifices in their lives to achieve this. So I have included a few members of the Leeds United Family that I know personally. These people are just a sample of the wider fanbase.

Some of them buy a new United shirt every year, some wear shirts from previous unsuccessful campaigns as badges of honour and some don't wear their colours at all. The point that I am making is that this is not an exclusive club, everybody is welcome and I am proud to be a part of it.

**Steve Chatterton**

*"I was born in Fareham, Hampshire, but now live in Northallerton. When I was about eight years old, the family moved to Leeds.*

*I am a season ticket holder at Elland Road and often travel down to the match on my motorbike. I went to my first match in 1965 when Mike O'Grady made his debut for United against Northampton Town. Leeds won 6-1! I was only 12 and went with my Dad.*

*Promotion means a lot to me, in sport and in life you get knocked down and suffer bad times as well as enjoying the good times. It teaches us all, especially young people to keep trying.*

*Many supporters were only children sixteen years ago so it's a very exciting time for the thousands of fans who have never experienced the Premier League. Bielsa is a teacher and a private person. The players all say that they have improved since working with him.*

*The fact that he avoids speaking English in his interviews just reinforces his need for privacy. Nevertheless he is down to earth and can communicate at every level.*

*I think the Whites will do as well as Sheffield United or Wolves next season and finish somewhere between 6th and 11th place. I expect there to be some investment in new players and believe that United will never get relegated again."*

## Alan Brown & Dave Ledgard

*"I was born in Bramley, but now live in Middleton. My first visit to Elland Road was on 26th February 1977 when we beat Manchester City 1-0 in the FA Cup. At the moment I am feeling happiness, relief and sadness.*

*Happy to be back at the top table of English Football. I'm feeling relief that we have come through the nightmare that we have been suffering for the last sixteen years. But I'm also sad that we have lost so many friends and heroes who didn't get to experience this with us.*

*I love Bielsa for what he has done for our club. The football over the last two years has been a joy to watch. I'm cautiously optimistic for the future as I think that we will surprise a lot of people with our brand of football."*

-Alan Brown

*"I was born in Dewsbury and live in Liversedge. My first game was against Manchester City in October 1971. We won 3-0.*

*I am extremely happy and it's been a relief in a funny sort of a way because the longer that we have been out of the Premier League, the further behind we've been getting. I believe that Marcelo Bielsa has the potential to be our greatest ever manager if his age doesn't get in the way.*

*I think that we will do quite well in the Premier League with our style of play, supplemented with a few signings to strengthen the squad."*

-Dave Ledgard

## Martyn Haunch & Don Deedigan

*"I was born in Leeds and still live in the city. The first game I went to was Everton at home in 1977 when United won 3-1.*

*Leeds are now back where they should be and I'm looking forward to seeing them take on the so-called 'big boys' in the cauldron of Elland Road. Bielsa is a humble guy who is clearly revered by the top managers in the game. He is held in the highest regard by his players and backroom staff.*

*He has given the Leeds fans exciting football to watch while continuing to improve a relatively small squad to become champions.*

*It is important that Bielsa gives those players that got Leeds back into the Premier League the opportunity to prove themselves at this level. Obviously there will be the need to add three or four new players, but I think if we do this we will be fine and can build towards being back in the Champions League."*

-Martyn Haunch

*"I was born and brought up in Leeds and still live there. The first game I ever went to was Leeds against Anderlecht. This was a 4-0 win for United and I can still remember it.*

*Bielsa is a genius and I'm looking forward to the Premier League. It will be great for the youngsters to see the big hitters at Elland Road again. I also think that with a bit of luck, we should finish in the top twelve."*

-Don Deedigan

**Mike Powell**

*"I was born in Wales but I now live in Hitchin, Hertfordshire. My first visit to Elland Road was in 1990 when I saw Leeds beat Norwich City 3-0.*

*My current feelings are of elation and relief at the end of years of disappointment and frustration. It is a feeling that we are back where we belong.*

*Marcelo Bielsa means everything to me as a Leeds Supporter. Together with the owner he has brought pride and respect to the club. I feel sure that his legacy will be felt for years to come.*

*I am confident that we will prosper now that we are a properly run football club. The first season will probably be one of consolidation, but after three seasons there is no reason why we shouldn't be competing in the top six."*

## Mark Lazell

"I *was born in Bedford and have lived there all my life. My first game was in 1977 at Highbury where we drew 1-1 with Arsenal. Gordon McQueen was the scorer. Being promoted means everything to me, it's great to be back in the top league.*

*Bielsa is a miracle worker, he has turned average players into a team who have been at the top of their game for two seasons.*

*I think they will perform admirably in the Premier League and introduce a breath of fresh air with 'Bielsaball'. We should easily finish in the top ten.*"

# Chapter Fourteen
## Conclusion

This book began with the feelings of loss and devastation after the play off defeat to Derby. Once this period of mourning was over, almost everyone was fixated on how United could secure the services of Bielsa for another season to finish the job.

Here hangs the clue. In the crazy world of modern football, many managers are not even given a whole season to achieve their objectives, never mind two.

From the beginning, Bielsa set up his plans to endure far longer than a single season. The infrastructure was changed from top to bottom but above all, the relationship and mutual respect between the Owner and Head Coach was key to the success that followed.

For me, there were two defining events of the season. The first was the eleven game unbeaten run which followed the defeats to Millwall and Charlton in the autumn. The second was the fifteen game sequence which concluded the campaign. After losing to Nottingham Forest in February, the Whites went on to win twelve games and draw two.

This remarkable run was only spoiled by the Cardiff City defeat, when hostilities resumed in June.

The lessons had been learned from the previous season and no amount of pressure from West Bromwich Albion, Fulham or Brentford could shake this Leeds United side off course.

The following players all made a significant contribution to United's league success this season.

**Ben White          46 Starts (46 Appearances)**
His silky skills and growing confidence made you wonder why we were worried about losing Jansson.

**Jack Harrison          45 Starts (46 Appearances)**
Was determined to improve his game and he did just that, scoring six goals and providing eight assists.

**Mateusz Klich          45 Starts (45 Appearances)**
Dependable and hard working, the Polish midfielder often doesn't get full recognition for his efforts.

**Stuart Dallas          45 Starts (45 Appearances)**
Another player who has blossomed under Bielsa's guidance. The Irishman is tenacious and versatile.

**Patrick Bamford          43 Starts (45 Appearances)**
Tireless, unselfish and tough enough to withstand the often unfair criticism of his scoring abilities.

**Kalvin Phillips          37 Starts (37 Appearances)**
A young leader who has become an integral part of Bielsa's side, with his feet firmly on the ground.

**Liam Cooper**      **36 Starts (38 Appearances)**
One of the most improved players under Bielsa. He has led by example both on and off the pitch.

**Kiko Casilla**      **36 Starts (36 Appearances)**
Played his part before a lengthy suspension, he's a brilliant shot stopper but is prone to a costly error.

**Luke Ayling**      **35 Starts (37 Appearances)**
His inspiring 'never say die' performances always made him an obvious choice to deputise as captain.

**Helder Costa**      **33 Starts (43 Appearances)**
Took time to settle in, but the midfielder has grown in stature as the season has progressed.

**Pablo Hernandez**      **27 Starts (36 Appearances)**
A stylist with his goals, assists and range of passes, he makes a mockery of his age with his stamina.

**Gjanni Alioski**      **21 Starts (39 Appearances)**
Has bags of enthusiasm and never gives in. His eccentric antics often provide light relief for us all.

**Gaetano Berardi**      **13 Starts (22 Appearances)**
A fans favourite who's sorted out his disciplinary record without losing any of his competitive edge.

**Tyler Roberts**      **12 Starts (23 Appearances)**
A versatile attacker. If he can steer clear of injuries, you feel that he'll be able to his fulfil his potential.

**Illan Meslier**          **10 Starts (10 Appearances)**
Grabbed his chance with both hands. He's cool under pressure and has excellent distribution.

**Barry Douglas**          **6 Starts (15 Appearances)**
The Scotsman spent much of the season on the treatment table, but was reliable when called upon.

**Adam Forshaw**          **6 Starts (7 Appearances)**
Made a great start to the season, but played no further part after an untimely injury.

**Jamie Shackleton**          **5 Starts (22 Appearances)**
Another promising youngster. His goals against Derby and Charlton will do him no harm at all.

**Eddie Nketiah**          **2 Starts (17 Appearances)**
Scored some important goals and has since proved his quality by being a regular in the Arsenal side.

**Pascal Struijk**          **2 Starts (5 Appearances)**
Broke in the side towards the end of the season. He's strong and steady on the ball.

**Ian Poveda**          **1 Start (4 Appearances)**
A skilful winger that started to come into his own during the concluding matches of the season.

All of these individuals were good players before they came into contact with Marcelo Bielsa but under his influence, they have joined together as a potent force who should have nothing to fear in the Premier League.

There are though, the pundits and so-called 'experts' who are already offering their advice to the Whites before they rejoin the elite.

"Bielsa will have to sign some big names."
"Bamford isn't good enough."
"They need more players with Premier League experience."

Most of the people who make these kind of statements still don't get it. As long as United can keep Marcelo Bielsa and his team, they will be fine. HE will decide what they need.

Once again Marcelo, a heartfelt muchas gracias for what you've delivered at Leeds United.

I am indebted to my grandson, George Gill, for his editing skills but also for his companionship.